INTRODUCING
ISSUES WITH
OPPOSING
VIEWPOINTS®

Marijuana

Noël Merino, *Book Editor*

GREENHAVEN PRESS
A part of Gale, Cengage Learning

GALE
CENGAGE Learning™

Detroit • New York • San Francisco • New Haven, Conn • Waterville, Maine • London

Elizabeth Des Chenes, *Managing Editor*

For more information, contact:
Greenhaven Press
27500 Drake Rd.
Farmington Hills, MI 48331-3535
Or you can visit our Internet site at gale.cengage.com

For product information and technology assistance, contact us at

Gale Customer Support, 1-800-877-4253
For permission to use material from this text or product, submit all requests online at www.cengage.com/permissions

Further permissions questions can be e-mailed to permissionrequest@cengage.com

Cover image © sydcinema/Shutterstock.com.

LIBRARY OF CONGRESS CATALOGING-IN-PUBLICATION DATA

Marijuana / Noël Merino, book editor.
    p. cm. -- (Introducing issues with opposing viewpoints)
  Includes bibliographical references and index.
  ISBN 978-0-7377-5683-8 (hardcover)
  1. Marijuana--United States. 2. Marijuana--Therapeutic use. 3. Marijuana--Law and legislation--United States. I. Merino, Noël.
  RM666.C266M364 2011
  362.29'50973--dc22

                                                                          2011014465

Printed in the United States of America
1 2 3 4 5 6 7 15 14 13 12 11

Contents

Chapter 3: Should Marijuana Be Legalized?

Foreword

I ndulging in a wide spectrum of ideas, beliefs, and perspectives is a critical cornerstone of democracy. After all, it is often debates over differences of opinion, such as whether to legalize abortion, how to treat prisoners, or when to enact the death penalty, that shape our society and drive it forward. Such diversity of thought is frequently regarded as the hallmark of a healthy and civilized culture. As the Reverend Clifford Schutjer of the First Congregational Church in Mansfield, Ohio, declared in a 2001 sermon, "Surrounding oneself with only like-minded people, restricting what we listen to or read only to what we find agreeable is irresponsible. Refusing to entertain doubts once we make up our minds is a subtle but deadly form of arrogance." With this advice in mind, Introducing Issues with Opposing Viewpoints books aim to open readers' minds to the critically divergent views that comprise our world's most important debates.

Introducing Issues with Opposing Viewpoints simplifies for students the enormous and often overwhelming mass of material now available via print and electronic media. Collected in every volume is an array of opinions that captures the essence of a particular controversy or topic. Introducing Issues with Opposing Viewpoints books embody the spirit of nineteenth-century journalist Charles A. Dana's axiom: "Fight for your opinions, but do not believe that they contain the whole truth, or the only truth." Absorbing such contrasting opinions teaches students to analyze the strength of an argument and compare it to its opposition. From this process readers can inform and strengthen their own opinions, or be exposed to new information that will change their minds. Introducing Issues with Opposing Viewpoints is a mosaic of different voices. The authors are statesmen, pundits, academics, journalists, corporations, and ordinary people who have felt compelled to share their experiences and ideas in a public forum. Their words have been collected from newspapers, journals, books, speeches, interviews, and the Internet, the fastest growing body of opinionated material in the world.

Introducing Issues with Opposing Viewpoints shares many of the well-known features of its critically acclaimed parent series, Opposing Viewpoints. The articles are presented in a pro/con format, allowing readers to absorb divergent perspectives side by side. Active reading questions preface each viewpoint, requiring the student to approach the material thoughtfully and carefully. Useful charts, graphs, and cartoons supplement each article. A thorough introduction provides readers with crucial background on an issue. An annotated bibliography points the reader toward articles, books, and websites that contain additional information on the topic. An appendix of organizations to contact contains a wide variety of charities, nonprofit organizations, political groups, and private enterprises that each hold a position on the issue at hand. Finally, a comprehensive index allows readers to locate content quickly and efficiently.

Introducing Issues with Opposing Viewpoints is also significantly different from Opposing Viewpoints. As the series title implies, its presentation will help introduce students to the concept of opposing viewpoints and learn to use this material to aid in critical writing and debate. The series' four-color, accessible format makes the books attractive and inviting to readers of all levels. In addition, each viewpoint has been carefully edited to maximize a reader's understanding of the content. Short but thorough viewpoints capture the essence of an argument. A substantial, thought-provoking essay question placed at the end of each viewpoint asks the student to further investigate the issues raised in the viewpoint, compare and contrast two authors' arguments, or consider how one might go about forming an opinion on the topic at hand. Each viewpoint contains sidebars that include at-a-glance information and handy statistics. A Facts About section located in the back of the book further supplies students with relevant facts and figures.

Following in the tradition of the Opposing Viewpoints series, Greenhaven Press continues to provide readers with invaluable exposure to the controversial issues that shape our world. As John Stuart Mill once wrote: "The only way in which a human being can make some approach to knowing the whole of a subject is by hearing what can be said about it by persons of every variety of opinion and studying all modes in which it can be looked at by every character of mind. No wise man ever acquired his wisdom in any mode but this." It is to this principle that Introducing Issues with Opposing Viewpoints books are dedicated.

Introduction

"In most of California's coastal metropolitan areas, marijuana is effectively legal today."

— Roger Parloff, "How Marijuana Became Legal"

In November of 2010 California voters defeated Proposition 19, the Regulate, Control, and Tax Cannabis Act of 2010. The act would have allowed adults aged twenty-one and older in California to possess, cultivate, and transport marijuana for personal use, permitting local governments to regulate and tax the commercial production and sale of marijuana. According to the California secretary of state, 53.5 percent of California voters turned down Proposition 19, with only 46.5 percent voting for the measure. Proponents of the ballot initiative intend to try again in 2012 for marijuana legalization, but some would argue that marijuana already *is* legal for all adults in California through the state's lax medical marijuana policy.

California was the first state to implement a law legalizing marijuana for medical use. Proposition 215, the Compassionate Use Act of 1996, was passed by California voters on November 5, 1996, with over 55 percent of voters approving. The proposition removed state-level criminal penalties on the use, possession, and cultivation of marijuana by patients, where such use "has been recommended by a physician who has determined that the person's health would benefit from the use of marijuana." The California legislature passed Senate Bill 420, effective January 1, 2004, which put into place guidelines for the legal use of medical marijuana in California. Among other regulations, the bill created a voluntary identification card program for qualified medical-marijuana users and a limit on marijuana possession. In addition, the bill allowed patients to "cultivate marijuana for medical purposes" through nonprofit collectives or cooperatives, though such marijuana transactions are subject to sales tax.

Even though legal use of marijuana in California is limited to medical purposes, many have noted that any resident eighteen and older can find a doctor to write a prescription. As journalist Roger Parloff notes, "Doctors seemingly eager to write such notes, typically in exchange for a $200 consultation fee, advertise in newspapers and on websites." Furthermore, there is no legal restriction in California on the types of medical conditions that marijuana can be used to treat, with the law noting a series of conditions and then adding, "any other illness for which marijuana provides relief." Because of this, Parloff says, "California doctors are authorizing patients to take marijuana to relieve such ailments as anxiety, headache, premenstrual syndrome, and trouble sleeping."[1] For this reason, marijuana is essentially legal for anyone willing to find a doctor who will write a recommendation.

Controversy in California has not centered on misuse of the law so much as on the existence of medical marijuana dispensaries. In a 2009 white paper, the California Police Chiefs Association claims, "Marijuana dispensaries are commonly large money-making enterprises that will sell marijuana to most anyone who produces a physician's written recommendation for its medical use." The association expressed concern that the dispensaries "have been tied to organized criminal gangs, foster large grow operations, and are often multimillion-dollar profit centers."[2] Marijuana dispensaries flourished in Los Angeles from 2007 to 2009, when the number of medical marijuana dispensaries had grown to over eight hundred.

Michael Larsen, president of the Eagle Rock Neighborhood Council, has been waging a fight for several years to cut the number of dispensaries allowed in his Los Angeles neighborhood, after the number of dispensaries in Eagle Rock grew to over twenty. The Los Angeles City Council approved an ordinance in January 2010 to cap the number of permitted dispensaries within the city at seventy and placed restrictions on where the dispensaries may be located. In June of 2010 the city began cracking down on dispensaries that were not legally registered, and the number of dispensaries started dropping, but Larsen says that many of the dispensaries in his neighborhood stayed open or reopened. He expressed frustration in August 2010, stating, "There's no enforcement and there seems to be nothing anyone can do about it."[3] In January 2011 it was reported that the Eagle

Rock Neighborhood Council was considering asking US attorney general Eric Holder to step in.

State legislation allowing use of medical marijuana does not undo federal legislation restricting the use of marijuana. The 1970 Controlled Substances Act (CSA) established a federal regulatory system designed to combat recreational drug abuse by making it unlawful to manufacture, distribute, dispense, or possess marijuana and other drugs. "California did not 'legalize' medical marijuana, but instead exercised the state's reserved powers to not punish certain marijuana offenses under state law when a physician has recommended its use to treat a serious medical condition."[4] The tension between state laws and federal law continues to cause confusion and debate about whether states have the power to legalize medical marijuana and whether the federal government should intervene. Although the US Department of Justice in 2009 stated an intent to stop raids on medical marijuana dispensaries in states where they are allowed (as of January 2011 fifteen states plus the District of Columbia allow the use of medical marijuana), this contradiction between state and federal law may need to be formally resolved.

The failure of Proposition 19 in California does not mean that the legalization issue in California is over. Stephen Gutwillig, state director of the pro-legalization Drug Policy Alliance, says, "This issue is not going anywhere and is likely to be stronger because this debate has placed reforming failed marijuana laws squarely in the mainstream political discourse."[5] Regardless, even without formal legalization, there are a host of issues involving the regulation of medical marijuana in California that will likely continue to create controversy. The issues of whether marijuana should be legal, for medical or recreational use, and how marijuana should be regulated by the government are just a few of the fascinating debates about marijuana explored in *Introducing Issues with Opposing Viewpoints: Marijuana.*

Notes

1. Roger Parloff, "How Marijuana Became Legal," *Fortune*, September 28, 2009, p. 140. http://money.cnn.com/2009/09/11/magazines/fortune/medical_marijuana_legalizing.fortune/.

2. California Police Chiefs Association's Task Force on Marijuana Dispensaries, "White Paper on Marijuana Dispensaries," April 22, 2009. www.californiapolicechiefs.org/nav_files/marijuana_files/files/MarijuanaDispensariesWhitePaper_042209.pdf.

3. Dennis Romero and Steve La, "Eagle Rock Pot Shops Stay Open Despite Order from L.A. to Close," *LA Weekly*, August 23, 2010. http://blogs.laweekly.com/informer/2010/08/eagle_rock_pot_shops.php.

4. Edmund G. Brown Jr., "Guidelines for the Security and Non-diversion of Marijuana Grown for Medical Use," August 2008. http://ag.ca.gov/cms_attachments/press/pdfs/n1601_medicalmarijuanaguidelines.pdf.

5. Dennis Romero, "What Killed Prop. 19?," *LA Weekly*, November 4, 2010. www.laweekly.com/2010-11-04/news/proposition-19-defeated-election-results-legalize-marijuana/.

Chapter 1

Is Marijuana Harmful?

Recent research into marijuana and its effects has heated up the controversy over its use.

Marijuana Is Harmful to Physical and Mental Health

Mark Porter

"The days are gone when sensible people argue that cannabis is harmless."

In the following viewpoint Mark Porter argues that research in recent years shows that marijuana is not harmless. Porter claims that although light marijuana use by most people is no more harmful than alcohol or cigarettes, heavy marijuana use and use by young people can cause more serious damage. Porter claims that research shows young people are particularly vulnerable to lung and brain damage. Porter contends that other research also suggests marijuana may harm the bones, impact sexual function, and increase the risk of testicular cancer. Porter is a general medical practitioner in England and a medical correspondent for the *Times*, a newspaper based in London, England.

AS YOU READ, CONSIDER THE FOLLOWING QUESTIONS:

1. What two legal drugs does the author claim harm more people in a weekend than marijuana does in a year?
2. How many marijuana joints a day does it take to do the same damage as twenty cigarettes a day, according to Porter?
3. As cited in the viewpoint, what fraction of marijuana users admits to having tried heroin?

I used to have fairly liberal views on cannabis [marijuana] and have compared it favourably in the past with alcohol and tobacco, both of which exact a bigger toll on our society than all illegal drugs combined.

But, along with most doctors, I have become increasingly concerned in recent years that the drug is much more dangerous than we thought, and certainly nowhere near as safe as most teenagers still think.

Increased Danger for Two Groups

The days are gone when sensible people argue that cannabis is harmless. The evidence that has been collected over the past decade shows that it is clearly not. . . . The vast majority are occasional users who, with time, will eventually turn their backs on the drug and emerge unscathed. This is in stark contrast to the outlook for the tens of millions who use cigarettes and alcohol—two legal drugs that kill, maim and injure more people in a weekend than cannabis does in a year. But there are two groups who seem particularly vulnerable to the harmful effects of cannabis: heavy users and those who used the drug at an early age.

Like all parents I like to think that my teenage daughters are sensible enough to avoid drugs, but I am realistic enough to know that if they haven't tried cannabis already then there is a good chance that they will. Statistics show that young children are almost as likely to experiment with cannabis as with tobacco. . . .

I have never been convinced that the legal status of cannabis makes any real difference to whether a teenager tries it. It has more to do with peer attitudes, and the overriding belief among teenagers today is that cannabis is a bit of harmless fun—the most dangerous thing about a joint being the tobacco that the grass or resin is mixed with. They are mistaken.

Dangers to the Lungs and Brain

Here are a few key facts that all teenagers (and their parents) should be made aware of.

Cannabis damages the lungs: Most people consider cannabis to be much safer than tobacco but, drag for drag, it is actually more harmful. Cannabis smoke is far more acrid than tobacco and causes more

Teenage brains seem to be particularly susceptible to the effects of marijuana. A recent study indicates that teen users under the age of fifteen are at greater risk of developing a serious mental illness in their twenties.

damage to the lining of the airways. The British Lung Foundation estimates that smoking an admittedly hefty three to four joints a day causes the same level of damage as smoking 20 cigarettes a day. And, like tobacco, it is packed with carcinogens [cancer-causing substances].

Chest physicians are reporting that a growing number of cannabis users appear to be developing the sort of lung damage normally seen only in middle-aged and elderly smokers—and up to 20 years earlier. And it doesn't seem to make much difference how you smoke it. Research into the relative "safety" of the various smoking devices—joints, bongs, vaporisers and water pipes—found no significant difference in the harmful chemicals inhaled.

Because water pipes filter out some of the ingredient (THC) that makes users high, they tend to inhale more of the harmful components to get a decent hit.

Cannabis can cause irreversible changes in the brain: The most alarming discovery in recent years has been that cannabis can trigger serious mental illness such as schizophrenia.

As a rough rule of thumb the average person's lifetime risk of developing schizophrenia is about one in 100. This risk increases to about one in 30 in occasional cannabis users and closer to one in 15 in regular users (at least once a day).

The brains of teenagers appear to be particularly susceptible to the drug. A recent study in New Zealand found that children who started to use cannabis before the age of 15 were nearly five times more likely to develop serious mental illness by their late twenties, compared with those who started

at 18. Neuroscientists suspect that the greater susceptibility of young teenagers is because the brain continues to develop during the teen years.

Drug use is thought to influence this final phase of brain formation, increasing the risk of the type of functional and chemical imbalances associated with conditions such as schizophrenia.

Potency and Addictiveness

The problem is compounded because most of the cannabis sold in Britain today is much more potent than that of a decade ago. These stronger variants (skunk) contain far more of THC, the active ingredient, which is thought to induce psychosis, and far less of another ingredient (cannabidiol) found in standard varieties, which is antipsychotic and protects the brain. But neurochemcal changes don't alter behaviour alone. Tests on mice suggest that they can also permanently disrupt a developing brain's ability to remember things, even after the drug is withdrawn. It is difficult to draw comparisons with human development, but scientists in the field believe that exposure before the age of 15 could cause lasting memory deficit.

Cannabis can be addictive: Contrary to street lore that you cannot become addicted to cannabis, one user in ten develops some form

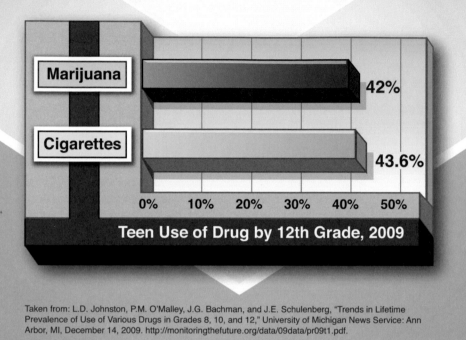

Teen Experimentation with Marijuana and Tobacco

Marijuana 42%

Cigarettes 43.6%

0% 10% 20% 30% 40% 50%

Teen Use of Drug by 12th Grade, 2009

Taken from: L.D. Johnston, P.M. O'Malley, J.G. Bachman, and J.E. Schulenberg, "Trends in Lifetime Prevalence of Use of Various Drugs in Grades 8, 10, and 12," University of Michigan News Service: Ann Arbor, MI, December 14, 2009. http://monitoringthefuture.org/data/09data/pr09t1.pdf.

of dependence, with abstinence leading to craving and withdrawal effects. . . .

Is it a gateway to more dangerous drugs? This is a controversial area. There is little doubt that cannabis users are more likely to try harder drugs such as cocaine and heroin, but this gateway effect is much smaller than we used to think. While most hard drug users start off trying cannabis, most cannabis users don't end up on hard drugs. Only one cannabis user in 25 admits to having tried heroin. That said, the social factors of mixing with peers who are using drugs and having access to supply can only make progression more likely. Age is again a factor—younger cannabis smokers are more likely to move on to hard drugs.

Recent Research Suggests Other Dangers

Cannabis and your bones: Recent work indicates that cannabis may accelerate the thinning of the skeleton that occurs as we age. Bone is a living tissue that is constantly being remodelled; cells called osteo-blasts lay down bone while osteoclasts dissolve it.

Careful balancing of the activities of both groups of cells mean that overall bone mass remains steady—at least until the age of 40—despite our entire skeleton being replaced every seven years.

Researchers from Aberdeen University have discovered that chemicals found in cannabis may upset this delicate balance in favour of the osteoclasts and bone resorption, leading to osteoporosis—a condition now thought to affect one woman in three, and one man in ten, over the age of 50.

Cannabis and sex: Little is known about the impact of cannabis on sexual function but there is growing anecdotal evidence that it may be linked to shrinking of the testicles and low sex drive in men.

Research published this week [February 9, 2009] suggests that it may increase the odds of developing testicular cancer. More research is needed but should any of these links be proved they could become the most powerful deterrent of all for boys and men.

Nothing in life is totally risk-free and all these potential hazards need to be put in context—the vast majority of people who try cannabis will come through the experience unscathed. But for some, particularly those who use it regularly, it will leave a permanent scar that could cost them their friends, family, career and possibly even their lives. At the moment we have no reliable way of identifying those most at risk but we do know that the earlier you start the more dangerous the drug is likely to be.

EVALUATING THE AUTHOR'S ARGUMENTS:

In this viewpoint Mark Porter compares marijuana to alcohol and tobacco. On this issue, is Porter's comparison more in line with that of Charles D. Stimson or David L. Nathan, authors of viewpoints later in this chapter? Explain your answer.

Viewpoint 2

Marijuana Is Not Harmful, and May Be Beneficial, to Brain Health

"Not only has modern science refuted the notion that marijuana is neurotoxic, recent scientific discoveries have indicated that cannabinoids are . . . neuro-protective."

Paul Armentano

In the following viewpoint Paul Armentano argues that recent research shows that marijuana is not harmful to the brain, and may improve brain health. Armentano points to studies that show positive outcomes on brain neurons after the administration of cannabinoids, the chemicals found in the marijuana plant. Armentano claims that research also shows that marijuana is a promising candidate for treatment of certain diseases, including cancer. Finally, he contends that despite the widespread belief to the contrary, recent studies support the conclusion that marijuana does not impair cognition and memory. Armentano is the deputy director of NORML (National Organization for the Reform of Marijuana Laws) and the NORML Foundation.

Paul Armentano, "Cannabis and the Brain: A User's Guide," National Organization for the Reform of Marijuana Laws (NORML), February 14, 2006. Reproduced by permission.

P reclinical data recently published in the *Journal of Clinical Investigation* demonstrating that cannabinoids [chemicals, some of which are found in marijuana,] may spur brain cell growth has reignited the international debate regarding the impact of marijuana on the brain. However, unlike previous pseudo-scientific campaigns that attempted to link pot smoking with a litany of cognitive abnormalities, modern research suggests what many cannabis [marijuana] enthusiasts have speculated all along: ganja [marijuana] is good for you.

Cannabinoids and Neurogenesis, the Birth of Neurons

"Study turns pot wisdom on its head," pronounced the [*Toronto*] *Globe and Mail* in October [2005]. News wires throughout North America and the world touted similar headlines—all of which were met with a monumental silence from federal officials and law enforcement. Why all the fuss? Researchers at the University of Saskatchewan in Saskatoon [Canada] found that the administration of synthetic cannabinoids in rats stimulated the proliferation of newborn neurons (nerve cells) in the hippocampus region of the brain and significantly reduced measures of anxiety and depression-like behavior. The results shocked researchers—who noted that almost all other so-called "drugs of abuse," including alcohol and tobacco, decrease neurogenesis in adults—and left the "pot kills brain cells" crowd with a platter of long-overdue egg on their faces.

While it would be premature to extrapolate the study's findings to humans, at a minimum, the data reinforce the notion that cannabinoids

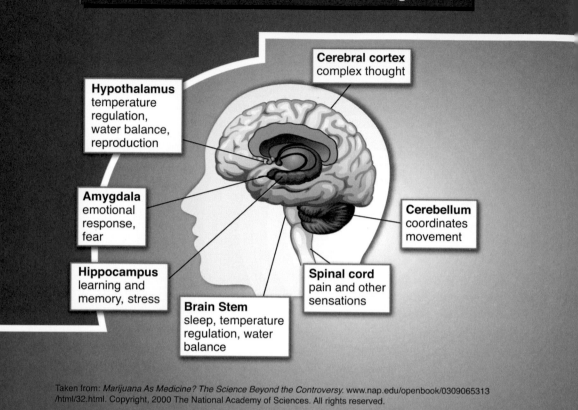

Locations and Functions of Brain Regions with Abundant Cannabinoid Receptors

Cerebral cortex
complex thought

Hypothalamus
temperature
regulation,
water balance,
reproduction

Amygdala
emotional
response,
fear

Cerebellum
coordinates
movement

Hippocampus
learning and
memory, stress

Spinal cord
pain and other
sensations

Brain Stem
sleep, temperature
regulation, water
balance

are unusually non-toxic to the brain and that even long-term use of marijuana likely represents little risk to brain function. The findings also offer further evidence that cannabinoids can play a role in the alleviation of depression and anxiety, and that cannabis-based medicines may one day offer a safer alternative to conventional anti-depressant pharmaceuticals such as Paxil and Prozac.

Cannabis and Neuroprotection, the Protection of Neurons

Not only has modern science refuted the notion that marijuana is neurotoxic, recent scientific discoveries have indicated that cannabinoids are, in fact, neuroprotective, particularly against alcohol-induced brain damage. In a recent preclinical study—the irony of which is obvious to anyone who reads it—researchers at the US National Institute of Mental Health (NIMH) reported that the administration of the non-psychoactive cannabinoid cannabidiol (CBD) reduced ethanol-induced cell death in the brain by up to 60 percent. "This study provides the first demonstration of CBD as an *in vivo* [within the living] neuroprotectant . . . in preventing binge ethanol-induced brain injury," the study's authors wrote in the May 2005 issue of the *Journal of Pharmacology and Experimental Therapeutics*. Alcohol poisoning is linked to hundreds of preventable deaths each year in the United States, according to the Centers for Disease Control [and Prevention], while cannabis cannot cause death by overdose.

Of course, many US neurologists have known about cannabis' neuroprotective prowess for years. NIMH scientists in 1998 first touted the ability of natural cannabinoids to stave off the brain-damaging effects of stroke and acute head trauma. Similar findings were then replicated by investigators in the Netherlands and Italy and, most recently, by a Japanese researcher in 2005. However, attempts to measure the potential neuroprotective effects of synthetic cannabinoid-derived medications in humans have so far been inconclusive.

> **FAST FACT**
>
> Marijuana is derived from the plant *Cannabis sativa*, which produces over 421 chemical compounds, including about 80 cannabinoids.

Cannabinoids and Treatment of Disease

Of all cancers, few are as aggressive and deadly as glioma. Glioma tumors quickly invade healthy brain tissue and are typically unresponsive to surgery and standard medical treatments. One agent they do respond to is cannabis.

Writing in the August 2005 issue of the *Journal of Neurooncology*, investigators at the California Pacific Medical Center Research Institute reported that the administration of THC [the psychoactive ingredient in marijuana] on human glioblastoma multiforme cell lines decreased the proliferation of malignant cells and induced apoptosis (programmed cell death) more rapidly than did the administration of the synthetic cannabis receptor agonist, WIN-55,212-2. Researchers also noted that THC selectively targeted malignant cells while ignoring healthy ones in a more profound manner than the synthetic alternative. Patients diagnosed with glioblastoma multiforme typically die within three months without therapy.

Previous research conducted in Italy has also demonstrated the capacity of CBD to inhibit the growth of glioma cells both *in vitro* (e.g., a petri dish) and in animals in a dose dependent manner. As a result, a Spanish research team is currently investigating whether the intracranial administration of cannabinoids can prolong the lives of patients diagnosed with inoperable brain cancer.

Most recently, a scientific analysis in the October issue of the journal *Mini-Reviews in Medicinal Chemistry* noted that, in addition to THC and CBD's brain cancer-fighting ability, studies have also shown cannabinoids to halt the progression of lung carcinoma, leukemia, skin carcinoma, colorectal cancer, prostate cancer and breast cancer.

Emerging evidence also indicates that cannabinoids may play a role in slowing the progression of certain neurodegenerative diseases, such as Multiple Sclerosis [MS], Parkinson's disease, Alzheimer's, and Amyotrophic Lateral Sclerosis [ALS] (a.k.a. Lou Gehrig's Disease). Recent animal studies have shown cannabinoids to delay disease progression and inhibit neurodegeneration in mouse models of ALS, Parkinson's, and MS. As a result, the *Journal of Neurological Sciences* recently pronounced, "There is accumulating evidence . . . to support the hypothesis that the cannabinoid system can limit the neurodegenerative processes that drive progressive disease," and patient trials investigating whether the use of oral THC and cannabis extracts may slow the progression of MS are now underway in the United Kingdom.

Marijuana's Impact on Cognition

But what about claims of cannabis' damaging effect on cognition? A review of the scientific literature indicates that rumors regarding the "stoner stupid" stereotype are unfounded. According to clinical trial data published this past spring [2005] in the *American Journal of Addictions*, cannabis use—including heavy, long-term use of the drug—has, at most, only a negligible impact on cognition and memo-

A multiple sclerosis (MS) patient uses a water pipe to smoke marijuana. Emerging evidence indicates that marijuana slows the progression of certain neurodegenerative diseases, including MS.

ry. Researchers at Harvard Medical School performed magnetic resonance imaging on the brains of 22 long-term cannabis users (reporting a mean of 20,100 lifetime episodes of smoking) and 26 controls (subjects with no history of cannabis use). Imaging displayed "no significant differences" between heavy cannabis smokers compared to controls, the study found.

Previous trials tell a similar tale. An October 2004 study published in the journal *Psychological Medicine* examining the potential long-term residual effects of cannabis on cognition in monozygotic [identical] male twins reported "an absence of marked long-term residual effects of marijuana use on cognitive abilities." A 2003 meta-analysis published in the *Journal of the International Neuropsychological Society* also "failed to reveal a substantial, systematic effect of long-term, regular cannabis consumption on the neurocognitive functioning of users who were not acutely intoxicated," and a 2002 clinical trial published in the *Canadian Medical Association Journal* determined, "Marijuana does not have a long-term negative impact on global intelligence."

Finally, a 2001 study published in the journal *Archives of General Psychiatry* found that long-term cannabis smokers who abstained from the drug for one week "showed virtually no significant differences from control subjects (those who had smoked marijuana less than 50 times in their lives) on a battery of 10 neuropsychological tests." Investigators further added, "Former heavy users, who had consumed little or no cannabis in the three months before testing, [also] showed no significant differences from control subjects on any of these tests on any of the testing days."

EVALUATING THE AUTHOR'S ARGUMENTS:

In this viewpoint Paul Armentano claims that recent studies support the view that marijuana is good for brain health. What study would Mark Porter, author of the previous viewpoint, cite as an objection to Armentano's claim?

Marijuana Is Much More Harmful than Alcohol

Charles D. Stimson

"Compared to alcohol, marijuana is not safe."

In the following viewpoint Charles D. Stimson contends that it is false that marijuana is no more dangerous than alcohol. Stimson contends that the historical policies of cultures show that some alcohol use has almost always been tolerated, whereas marijuana use has rarely been tolerated. Stimson claims that this is because marijuana is more addictive than alcohol, is usually consumed to the point of intoxication, and is harmful to health. Stimson concludes that just because there are drugs even more harmful than marijuana does not mean that it is similar to the legal drug alcohol or that legalizing marijuana should be reconsidered. Stimson is a senior legal fellow at the Heritage Foundation and an instructor at the Naval Justice School in Newport, Rhode Island.

Charles D. Stimson, "Legalizing Marijuana: Why Citizens Should Just Say No," Legal Memorandum, September 13, 2010. Reproduced by permission from The Heritage Foundation.

Marijuana advocates have had some success peddling the notion that marijuana is a "soft" drug, similar to alcohol, and fundamentally different from "hard" drugs like cocaine or heroin. It is true that marijuana is not the most dangerous of the commonly abused drugs, but that is not to say that it is safe. Indeed, marijuana shares more in common with the "hard" drugs than it does with alcohol.

An Argument for Marijuana Legalization

A common argument for legalization is that smoking marijuana is no more dangerous than drinking alcohol and that prohibiting the use of marijuana is therefore no more justified than the prohibition of alcohol. As Jacob Sullum, author of *Saying Yes: In Defense of Drug Use*, writes:

> Americans understood the problems associated with alcohol abuse, but they also understood the problems associated with Prohibition, which included violence, organized crime, official corruption, the erosion of civil liberties, disrespect for the law, and injuries and deaths caused by tainted black-market booze. They decided that these unintended side effects far outweighed whatever harms Prohibition prevented by discouraging drinking. The same sort of analysis today would show that the harm caused by drug prohibition far outweighs the harm it prevents, even without taking into account the value to each individual of being sovereign over his own body and mind.

At first blush, this argument is appealing, especially to those wary of over-regulation by government. But it overlooks the enormous difference between alcohol and marijuana.

Legalization advocates claim that marijuana and alcohol are mild intoxicants and so should be regulated similarly; but as the experience of nearly every culture, over the thousands of years of human history, demonstrates, alcohol is different. Nearly every culture has its own alcoholic preparations, and nearly all have successfully regulated alcohol consumption through cultural norms. The same cannot be said of marijuana. There are several possible explanations for alcohol's unique status: For most people, it is not addictive; it is rarely consumed to the point of intoxication; low-level consumption is consistent with most manual and intellectual tasks; it has several positive health benefits; and it is formed by the fermentation of many common substances and easily metabolized by the body.

To be sure, there are costs associated with alcohol abuse, such as drunk driving and disease associated with excessive consumption. A few

A PET scan of the brains of a marijuana user, bottom, and a nonmarijuana user, top. Marijuana reduces brain activity in the cerebellum, shown in red, and affects cognitive abilities.

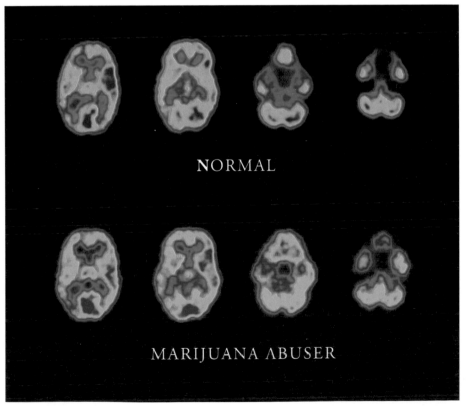

cultures—and this nation for a short while during Prohibition—have concluded that the benefits of alcohol consumption are not worth the costs. But they are the exception; most cultures have concluded that it is acceptable in moderation. No other intoxicant shares that status.

Differences Between Alcohol and Marijuana

Alcohol differs from marijuana in several crucial respects. First, marijuana is far more likely to cause addiction. Second, it is usually consumed to the point of intoxication. Third, it has no known general healthful properties, though it may have some palliative effects. Fourth, it is toxic and deleterious to health. Thus, while it is true that both alcohol and marijuana are less intoxicating than other mood-altering drugs, that is not to say that marijuana is especially similar to alcohol or that its use is healthy or even safe.

In fact, compared to alcohol, marijuana is not safe. Long-term, moderate consumption of alcohol carries few health risks and even offers some significant benefits. For example, a glass of wine (or other alcoholic drink) with dinner actually improves health. Dozens of peer-reviewed medical studies suggest that drinking moderate amounts of alcohol reduces the risk of heart disease, strokes, gallstones, diabetes, and death from a heart attack. According to the Mayo Clinic, among many others, moderate use of alcohol (defined as two drinks a day) "seems to offer some health benefits, particularly for the heart." Countless articles in medical journals and other scientific literature confirm the positive health effects of moderate alcohol consumption.

> **FAST FACT**
>
> The National Institute on Drug Abuse claims that long-term marijuana abusers trying to quit report withdrawal symptoms including irritability, sleeplessness, decreased appetite, anxiety, and drug craving.

The effects of regular marijuana consumption are quite different. For example, the National Institute on Drug Abuse (a division of the National Institutes of Health) has released studies showing that use of marijuana has wide-ranging negative health effects. Long-term marijuana consumption "impairs the ability of T-cells in the lungs'

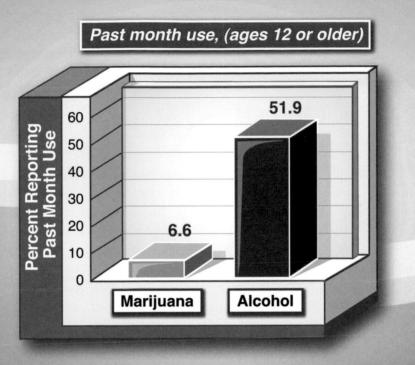

Current Uses of Marijuana and Alcohol in the General Population, 2009

Past month use, (ages 12 or older)

Percent Reporting Past Month Use

Marijuana: 6.6
Alcohol: 51.9

Taken from: SAMHSA, *2009 National Survey on Drug Use and Health* (September 2010).

immune system to fight off some infections." These studies have also found that marijuana consumption impairs short-term memory, making it difficult to learn and retain information or perform complex tasks; slows reaction time and impairs motor coordination; increases heart rate by 20 percent to 100 percent, thus elevating the risk of heart attack; and alters moods, resulting in artificial euphoria, calmness, or (in high doses) anxiety or paranoia. And it gets worse: Marijuana has toxic properties that can result in birth defects, pain, respiratory system damage, brain damage, and stroke.

Further, prolonged use of marijuana may cause cognitive degradation and is "associated with lower test scores and lower educational attainment because during periods of intoxication the drug affects the ability to learn and process information, thus influencing attention, concentration, and short-term memory." Unlike alcohol, marijuana has been shown to have a residual effect on cognitive ability that persists beyond the period of intoxication. According to the National Institute on Drug Abuse, whereas alcohol is broken down relatively quickly in the human body, THC (tetrahydrocannabinol, the main active chemical in marijuana) is stored in organs and fatty tissues, allowing it to remain in a user's body for days or even weeks after consumption. Research has shown that marijuana consumption may also cause "psychotic symptoms."

The Harmful Effects of Marijuana

Marijuana's effects on the body are profound. According to the British Lung Foundation, "smoking three or four marijuana joints is as bad for your lungs as smoking twenty tobacco cigarettes." Researchers in Canada found that marijuana smoke contains significantly higher levels of numerous toxic compounds, like ammonia and hydrogen cyanide, than regular tobacco smoke. In fact, the study determined that ammonia was found in marijuana smoke at levels of up to 20 times the levels found in tobacco. Similarly, hydrogen cyanide was found in marijuana smoke at concentrations three to five times greater than those found in tobacco smoke.

Marijuana, like tobacco, is addictive. One study found that more than 30 percent of adults who used marijuana in the course of a year were dependent on the drug. These individuals often show signs of withdrawal and compulsive behavior. Marijuana dependence is also responsible for a large proportion of calls to drug abuse help lines and treatment centers.

To equate marijuana use with alcohol consumption is, at best, uninformed and, at worst, actively misleading. Only in the most superficial ways are the two substances alike, and they differ in every way that counts: addictiveness, toxicity, health effects, and risk of intoxication.

EVALUATING THE AUTHOR'S ARGUMENTS:

In this viewpoint Charles D. Stimson argues against the view that marijuana is no more dangerous than alcohol. What is one way in which David L. Nathan, author of the next viewpoint, argues that alcohol is more dangerous?

Viewpoint

4

Marijuana Is No More Harmful than Currently Legal Substances

David L. Nathan

"Legal cannabis would never become the societal problem that alcohol already is."

In the following viewpoint David L. Nathan contends that marijuana should be legalized because of its similarity to other, legal recreational drugs. Nathan argues that alcohol is more dangerous than marijuana, yet is legal. Furthermore, Nathan claims that the prohibition of drugs such as alcohol and marijuana are greater than the costs of regulating them. Nathan believes that treating marijuana like alcohol and cigarettes is the only rational approach to the issue, which requires making all three drugs legal or all illegal. Nathan is a psychiatrist in Princeton, New Jersey, and a clinical associate professor at the Robert Wood Johnson Medical School of the University of Medicine and Dentistry of New Jersey.

AS YOU READ, CONSIDER THE FOLLOWING QUESTIONS:
1. Americans are wasting billions of dollars doing what, according to Nathan?
2. The author claims that which drug—alcohol or marijuana—frequently induces violent behavior and physiological dependence?
3. According to Nathan, in order to be consistent the prohibition of marijuana necessitates what?

Most Americans are paying too much for marijuana. I'm not referring to people who smoke it—using the drug generally costs about as much as using alcohol. Marijuana is unaffordable for the rest of America because billions are wasted on misdirected drug education and distracted law enforcement, and we also fail to tax the large underground economy that supplies cannabis.

On Monday [January 11, 2010], the New Jersey legislature passed a bill legalizing marijuana for a short list of medical uses. Outgoing Democratic Gov. Jon Corzine says he will sign it into law [which he did on January 18, 2010]. This is a positive step, as cannabis has several unique medical applications. But the debate over medical marijuana has obscured the larger issue of pot prohibition.

FAST FACT

The Eighteenth Amendment, prohibiting the production and consumption of alcohol in the United States, went into effect in 1920 until it was repealed in 1933 by the Twenty-First Amendment.

The Cost of Prohibition

As a psychiatrist, I treat individuals who often suffer from devastating substance abuse. Over many years of dealing with my patients' problems, I have come to realize that we are wasting precious resources on the fight against marijuana, which more closely resembles legal recreational drugs than illegal ones. My conscience compels me to support a comprehensive and nationwide decriminalization of marijuana.

Prohibition did decrease alcoholism and alcohol consumption in the 1920s. However, the resulting rise of violent organized crime and the loss of tax revenue were untenable and led to the repeal of Prohibition. By analogy, while the broad decriminalization of marijuana will likely reduce the societal and economic costs of pot prohibition, it could lead to more use and abuse.

Marijuana, Alcohol, and Other Drugs

The risks of marijuana use are mild compared to those of heroin, ecstasy and other illegal drugs, but the drug is not harmless. A small number of my patients cannot tolerate any use without serious impact on underlying disorders. Others become daily, heavy smokers, manifesting psychological if not physiological dependence. While most of my patients appear to suffer no ill effects from occasional use, the drug makes my work more difficult with certain individuals.

So why do I support decriminalization? First, marijuana prohibition doesn't prevent widespread use of the drug, although it does clog our legal system with a small percentage of users and dealers unlucky enough to be prosecuted. More to the point, legal cannabis would never become the societal problem that alcohol already is.

In most of my substance-abuse patients, I am far more concerned about their consumption of booze than pot. Alcohol frequently induces violent or dangerous behavior and often-irreversible physiological dependence; marijuana does neither. Chronic use of cannabis raises the

Alcohol intoxication can induce violent or dangerous behavior and irreversible physiological dependence; marijuana does not.

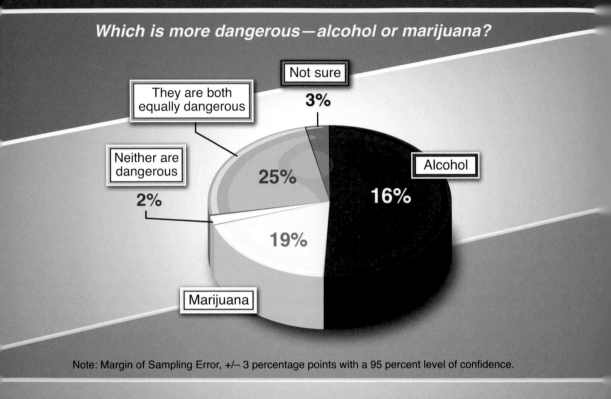

Which is more dangerous—alcohol or marijuana?

Not sure
3%

They are both equally dangerous
25%

Neither are dangerous
2%

Alcohol
16%

19%

Marijuana

Note: Margin of Sampling Error, +/– 3 percentage points with a 95 percent level of confidence.

Taken from: National Survey of 1,000 Adults Conducted August 26–27, 2009 by Rasmussen Reports.

risk of lung cancer, weight gain, and lingering cognitive changes—but chronic use of alcohol can cause pancreatitis, cirrhosis and permanent dementia. In healthy but reckless teens and young adults, it is frighteningly easy to consume a lethal dose of alcohol, but it is almost impossible to do so with marijuana. Further, compared with cannabis, alcohol can cause severe impairment of judgment, which results in greater concurrent use of hard drugs.

The Regulation of Legal Drugs

Many believe marijuana is a gateway drug—perhaps not so harmful in itself but one that leads to the use of more serious drugs. That is not borne out in practice, except that the illegal purchase of cannabis often exposes consumers to profit-minded dealers who push the hard stuff. In this way, the gateway argument is one in favor of decriminalization. If marijuana were purchased at liquor stores rather than on street corners where heroin and crack are also sold, there would likely be a decrease in the use of more serious drugs.

The nation badly needs the revenue of a "sin tax" on marijuana, akin to alcohol and tobacco taxes. Our government could also save money by ending its battle against marijuana in the drug war and redirecting funds to proactive drug education and substance-abuse treatment. Hyperbolic rants about the evils of marijuana could give way to realistic public education about the drug's true risks, such as driving under the influence.

Our nation can acknowledge the dangers of cigarettes, alcohol and marijuana while still permitting their use. The only logically and morally consistent argument for marijuana prohibition necessitates the criminalization of all harmful recreational drugs, including alcohol, nicotine and caffeine. We can agree that such an infringement on personal freedoms is as impractical as it is un-American. The time has come to accept that our nation's attitude toward marijuana has been misguided for generations and that the only rational approach to cannabis is to legalize, regulate and tax it.

EVALUATING THE AUTHOR'S ARGUMENTS:

In this viewpoint David L. Nathan claims that dangers of certain drugs can be acknowledged while also allowing a legal status. Do the other authors in this chapter agree or disagree with Nathan on this point?

Marijuana's Increased Strength Has Made It More Harmful

The Independent on Sunday

> *"Cannabis use is associated with growing mental health problems."*

In the following viewpoint the editorial staff of the *Independent on Sunday* retracts its previous position in favor of decriminalization of marijuana, claiming that new facts have made them reverse course. The *Independent on Sunday* argues that use of marijuana in recent years has shifted toward stronger forms of the drug. Additionally, the author argues that this stronger marijuana has created more psychological harms for the user. Although the author agrees that a social policy of focusing on education and treatment is better than extreme criminalization, the *Independent on Sunday* claims that full decriminalization should no longer be pursued because of the fact that marijuana is now more dangerous because of its increased strength. The *Independent on Sunday* is the Sunday edition of a newspaper published in the United Kingdom.

AS YOU READ, CONSIDER THE FOLLOWING QUESTIONS:
1. According to the author, what two shifts occurred to cause its change in position on marijuana?
2. The illegality of marijuana possession acts in what important way, according to the *Independent on Sunday*?
3. The *Independent on Sunday* contends that what policy toward marijuana is better than locking people up?

Yes, our front page today [March 18, 2007] is calculated to grab your attention. We do not really believe that *The Independent on Sunday* was wrong at the time, 10 years ago, when we called for cannabis [marijuana] to be decriminalised. As Rosie Boycott, who was the editor who ran the campaign, argues, the drug that she sought to decriminalize then was rather different from that which is available on the streets now.

The Marijuana Decriminalization Campaign

Indeed, this newspaper's campaign was less avant-garde than it seemed. Only four years later, *The Daily Telegraph* went farther, calling for cannabis to be legalised for a trial period. We were leading a consensus, which even this Government [of the United Kingdom]. . . could not resist, downgrading cannabis from class B to class C.

At the same time, however, two things were happening. One was the shift towards more powerful forms of the drug, known as skunk. The other was the emerging evidence of the psychological harm caused to a minority of users, especially teenage boys and particularly associated with skunk.

FAST FACT

In 2007 the Office of National Drug Control Policy announced that the increasing potency of marijuana may be leading to an increase in teen marijuana treatment admissions and emergency room visits.

We report today that the number of cannabis users on drug treatment programmes has risen 13-fold since our campaign was launched,

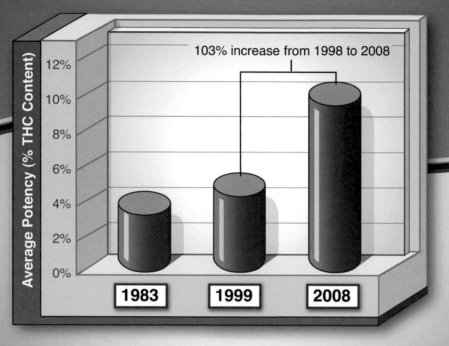

Potency of Seized Marijuana in the United States

103% increase from 1998 to 2008

Average Potency (% THC Content)

12%
10%
8%
6%
4%
2%
0%

1983 1999 2008

Taken from: Office of National Drug Control Policy, "Marijuana: Know the Facts," October 2010.

and that nearly half of the 22,000 currently on such programmes are under the age of 18. Of course, part of the explanation for this increase is that the provision of treatment is better than it was 10 years ago. But there is no question, as Robin Murray, one of the leading experts in this field, argues on these pages, that cannabis use is associated with growing mental health problems.

The Emphasis on Mental Health

Another campaign run—more recently—by this newspaper is to raise awareness of mental health issues and to press the Government to improve provision for those suffering from mental illnesses. The threat to mental health posed by cannabis has to take precedence over the liberal instinct that inspired Ms Boycott 10 years ago.

Many elements of her campaign remain valid today, however. The diversion of police resources into picking up easy convictions for cannabis possession was a waste. The rhetoric of the "war on drugs" tended to distort priorities: the current shift towards a strategy of harm reduction is a long overdue correction. Where we part company with her is on her view that the legalisation of all drugs is desirable because it would end the involvement of organised crime. So it might, but the fact that the possession of cannabis—and other drugs—is illegal acts as an important social restraint.

In fact, there is a strong case for believing that the present state of the law and of government policy is about right. The way the police enforce the law seems to be a reasonable compromise, while the emphasis of public policy is on information, education and treatment. The more the facts can be driven home about the differences between old-style hash and modern skunk, and about the risks to mental health, the better. And the more that policy towards drugs generally focuses on the causes of addictive or self-destructive behaviour, rather than locking people up, the better still.

Newer, more potent strains of marijuana have been linked to growing mental problems among teen boys.

A Change of Facts

The growing evidence of the risk of psychological harm posed by cannabis means that the time has come for us to reverse one of the positions with which—before the Iraq war—this newspaper was most identified.

We quote [economist] John Maynard Keynes in our defence: "When the facts change, I change my mind. What do you do, sir?"

> **EVALUATING THE AUTHOR'S ARGUMENTS:**
>
> In this viewpoint the *Independent on Sunday* claims that the increased strength of marijuana has made marijuana more dangerous. What would Jacob Sullum, author of the next viewpoint, say to dispute this?

There Is No Evidence That Marijuana's Increased Strength Has Made It More Harmful

"With stronger pot, people can smoke less to achieve the same effect."

Jacob Sullum

In the following viewpoint Jacob Sullum argues that the concerns raised by the Office of National Drug Control Policy (ONDCP) about the increased potency of marijuana are not supported by evidence. Sullum disputes the extent to which marijuana potency has risen but, regardless, denies that this is a bad thing. Claims that today's marijuana is more addictive, Sullum says, are not based in reality and are merely propaganda. Sullum concludes that ONDCP's worry about marijuana strength is not grounded in reality. Sullum is a senior editor at *Reason* magazine and Reason.com and a nationally syndicated columnist.

AS YOU READ, CONSIDER THE FOLLOWING QUESTIONS:
1. According to Sullum, the head of the Office of National Drug Control Policy (ONDCP) stated in 2002 that the potency of marijuana has increased by how many times?
2. Why does Sullum think that ONDCP should be praising the increased potency of marijuana?
3. Marijuana arrests have increased by what percent since 1990, according to the author?

According to federal drug czar John Walters [2001–2009], the marijuana available in the United States is better than ever. Well, that's not quite the way he put it, but it's closer to the truth.

The Claims About Marijuana Potency

Last week [June 2008], as part of its ongoing effort to convince baby boomers that today's "Pot 2.0" is much more dangerous than the stuff they smoked when they were young, Walters' Office of National Drug Control Policy (ONDCP) announced that "levels of THC—the psychoactive ingredient in marijuana—have reached the highest-ever amounts since scientific analysis of the drug began in the late 1970s." The University of Mississippi's Potency Monitoring Project reports that the average THC content of the seized marijuana it tests was 8.1 percent last year, up from 3.2 percent in 1983.

That increase is much less dramatic than the one Walters alleged a few years ago. In a 2002 *San Francisco Chronicle* op-ed piece, he asserted that "the potency of available marijuana has not merely 'doubled,' but increased as much as 30 times" since 1974, when "the average THC content of marijuana was less than 1 percent."

> **FAST FACT**
>
> *Reefer Madness* was a 1936 film about the dangers of marijuana and is considered today to be a cult classic because of its extreme demonization of the drug.

Various marijuana samples are tested at a lab in Denver, Colorado. Different strains of marijuana vary greatly in potency.

Since 1 percent is the threshold at which experimental subjects can detect a psychoactive effect, if Walters were right it would mean that people who smoked pot in the mid-'70s, when marijuana was even more popular than it is today, typically did not get high as a result. This rather implausible claim is based on a small, nonrepresentative sample of low-quality marijuana that probably degraded in storage.

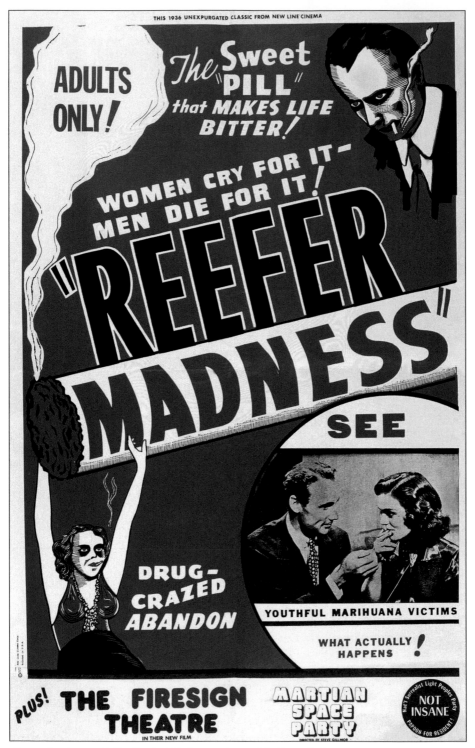

Poster for the 1936 film Reefer Madness, *directed by Louis J. Gasnier.*

Worse, to get his impressive 30-to-1 ratio, Walters compared the weakest pot of the '70s to the strongest pot of this decade. As a review of research on marijuana potency in the July 2008 issue of the journal *Addiction* notes, "There is enormous variation in potency, within a given year, from sample to sample," such that "cannabis users may be exposed to greater variation of cannabis potency in a single year . . . than over years or decades."

The Benefits of Stronger Marijuana

Even when the ONDCP is comparing annual averages, it's not clear that the government's samples, which depend on whose marijuana law enforcement agencies happen to seize, are comparable from year to year or representative of the U.S. market. Still, it's likely that average THC content has increased significantly during the last couple of decades as growers have become more adept at meeting the demands of increasingly discriminating consumers. The question is why Walters thinks that's a bad thing.

With stronger pot, people can smoke less to achieve the same effect, thereby reducing their exposure to combustion products, the most serious health risk associated with marijuana consumption. Yet the ONDCP inexplicably warns that higher THC levels could mean "an increased risk" of "respiratory problems."

A Self-Justifying Policy

It also trots out warnings about reefer madness reminiscent of anti-drug propaganda from the 1930s, conflating correlation (between heavy pot smoking and depression, for example) with causation. Nora Volkow, director of the National Institute on Drug Abuse, worries that stronger pot might be more addictive, although she concedes that "more research is needed to establish this link between higher THC potency and higher addiction risk." By contrast, the Australian scientists who wrote the *Addiction* article say "more research is needed to determine whether increased potency . . . translates to harm for users." Unlike our government, they are open to the possibility that the link Volkow seeks to establish does not in fact exist.

To bolster the idea that marijuana is more addictive today, the ONDCP notes that "16.1% of drug treatment admissions [in 2006] were for marijuana as the primary drug of abuse," compared to "6% in 1992." But referrals from the criminal justice system account for three-fifths of these treatment admissions, and marijuana arrests have increased by more than 150 percent since 1990.

By arresting people for marijuana possession and forcing them into treatment, the government shows why it has to arrest people for marijuana possession. That's our self-justifying drug policy in a nutshell.

EVALUATING THE AUTHOR'S ARGUMENTS:

In this viewpoint Jacob Sullum disputes some of the more extreme claims about marijuana potency. Does his conclusion rest on these claims being exaggerated? Why or why not?

Chapter 2

Should Marijuana Be Used as Medicine?

THC potency ratings for medical marijuana are displayed at an Oakland, California, medical marijuana clinic.

Medical Marijuana Should Be Legal

"The existing medical marijuana laws . . . have protected patients without causing problems for law enforcement or increasing drug abuse."

Joe Gamble

In the following viewpoint Joe Gamble argues that medical marijuana should be legalized. A resident of Liverpool, New York, Gamble encourages his state to take the action that several others have taken in allowing medical use of marijuana. Gamble claims that marijuana relieves some of the symptoms of his multiple sclerosis, and he uses it illegally. Gamble contends that states with medical marijuana laws have not had problems with increased crime or drug abuse. Furthermore, he claims that there is overwhelming popular support for legalizing medical marijuana. Gamble is a former US Army paratrooper and commercial pilot.

AS YOU READ, CONSIDER THE FOLLOWING QUESTIONS:
1. What medicine does the author claim has helped his symptoms the most?
2. Gamble claims that studies have confirmed that marijuana is helpful for what kind of pain?
3. According to the author, which two states have legalized medical marijuana by popular referendum?

Post-Standard (Syracuse, NY), April 24, 2009, for "Let This Be the Year for Medical Marijuana," by Joe Gamble. Reproduced by permission of the author.

Two years ago, at the age of 31, a diagnosis of multiple sclerosis [MS] turned the life I'd known upside-down and signaled an end to my career as a commercial pilot. Now, forced to break the law to have some semblance of a bearable existence, I am appealing to the New York State Legislature for help.

An Effective Medication

My career in the air began in the Army in 1993, where I was a paratrooper with the 1st Battalion 501st Arctic Parachute Infantry Regiment at Fort Richardson, Alaska. Since then, I've trained at flight schools and become an FAA [Federal Aviation Administration]-certified airline transport pilot. I've been a pilot for US Airways and flown corporate jets commercially for several different companies.

But now, at 33, I have had to relearn how to walk three times. My disease has progressed rapidly, and the pain—ranging from pins and needles to shooting pains throughout my body—never goes away. At times my arms and legs move on their own, twitching all over

At a medical marijuana rally in Texas, a man with multiple sclerosis (MS) advocates for legalization of the drug. Many MS sufferers must use marijuana illegally to relieve their symptoms.

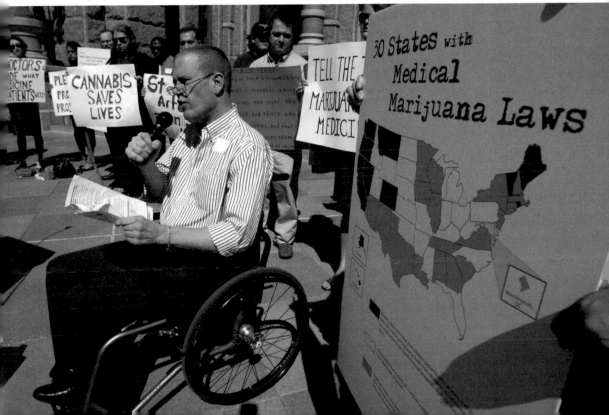

uncontrollably. I feel sick to my stomach frequently. Falling asleep is a chore. I've dropped 20 pounds due to the illness.

I've been on several different medications, but the help they give is limited. One medicine really does increase my appetite, ease the sick feeling in my stomach, help me fall asleep and calm the pain and twitching, but it's illegal: marijuana.

Laws About Medical Marijuana

So every day I am forced to break the laws of the state of New York in order to use the medicine that does the most to relieve the constant torture I've been condemned to live with. But it doesn't have to be this way.

Thirteen other states [as of April 2009]—home to one-quarter of the U.S. population—permit medical use of marijuana. These laws protect patients from criminal penalties if they use medical marijuana as recommended by a physician to treat MS, cancer, AIDS or other ailments that cause severe pain, nausea or vomiting.

In New York, medical marijuana legislation has passed our state Assembly twice, only to stall in the Senate. Now, identical bills—A.B. 7542 and S.B. 4041—have been introduced in the Assembly and Senate, and a change in Senate leadership has given us hope that 2009 will be the year that this simple, humane measure will finally become law. [As of May 2011, the bills had not been passed.]

> ## FAST FACT
>
> Ten states—Alabama, Connecticut, Idaho, Illinois, Massachusetts, New Hampshire, New York, North Carolina, Ohio, and Pennsylvania—have pending legislation to legalize medical marijuana as of May 2011.

All that is required is for our representatives in Albany to stand up and do what's right.

That medical marijuana is helpful for some patients who don't find relief from conventional medicines is no longer in question. Studies published in recent years have confirmed that it can be particularly helpful for what's known as neuropathic pain—pain caused by nerve damage, precisely the type of pain those of us with MS must endure.

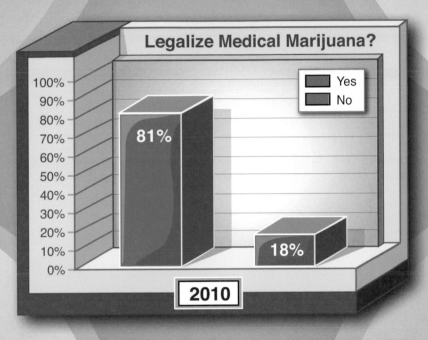

Legalize Medical Marijuana?

81%

18%

2010

Yes

No

Taken from: ABC News/*Washington Post* poll: Medical Marijuana Embargoed for Release After 5 p.m. Monday, January 18, 2010.

Support for Medical Marijuana

And it's clear that the existing medical marijuana laws—including those in nearby Vermont and Rhode Island—have protected patients without causing problems for law enforcement or increasing drug abuse.

Medical marijuana laws passed overwhelmingly by popular referendum in blue states like Michigan and red states like Montana. Here in New York, polling has shown overwhelming public support—including among registered Republicans and Conservatives.

But we don't have the ability to change state laws at the ballot box. If patients like me, simply seeking relief from the symptoms that haunt us every day, are ever to avoid living in fear, it will require our state legislators to stand up and protect us.

This should be the year. I don't want to be a criminal anymore.

Medical Marijuana Should Not Be Legal

William T. Breault

"The road that medical marijuana legislation is traveling is laden with potholes."

In the following viewpoint William T. Breault argues that marijuana should not be legalized for medicinal purposes. In response to Massachusetts's consideration of the issue, Breault warns that there are dangers in legalizing medical marijuana. In particular, Breault worries that allowing marijuana to be used as a medicine will increase use by minors. Breault claims that there is no justification for treating smokable marijuana as a medicine. He concludes that the conventional process for approving medications, through the US Food and Drug Administration (FDA), should be followed, and in this case the FDA does not approve. Breault is chairman of the Main South Alliance for Public Safety, a nonprofit organization in Worcester, Massachusetts.

AS YOU READ, CONSIDER THE FOLLOWING QUESTIONS:
1. Under the proposed Massachusetts medical marijuana bill, how many full-grown marijuana plants are permitted per patient?
2. What two FDA-approved drugs does the author claim should be used instead of smokable marijuana?
3. Breault claims that what professional group supports research into non-smokable forms of tetrahydrocannabinol, or THC?

The medical marijuana bill [The Massachusetts Medical Marijuana Act, HB 2160] will set up a medical marijuana program similar to the much abused one in California. Advocates claim medical marijuana will help seriously ill people with cancer, AIDS and glaucoma. But what is the reality? An analysis of medical marijuana patient records in California shows that 52 percent of the patients were between the ages of 17 and 30. In addition, 63 percent of the primary caregivers purchasing marijuana for the patients were between the ages of 18 and 30. Only 2 percent of customers obtained physician recommendations for AIDS, glaucoma or cancer. An extremely high number of people were using medical marijuana for insomnia, anxiety and depression.

> **FAST FACT**
>
> According to SAMHSA's 2008 National Survey on Drug Use and Health, the five states with the highest marijuana use among youth aged twelve to seventeen are Vermont, Rhode Island, New Hampshire, Colorado, and Maine.

Medical Marijuana and Kids

This legislation is reckless public policy. We empathize with the stories of those the bill's supporters claim would see relief, but we fear that Massachusetts would be making a mistake. The pitfalls associated with this policy are many and the opportunities for misuse and abuse are plentiful.

The medical marijuana bill permits huge amounts of crude marijuana to be smoked or eaten as medicine. Up to 12 full-grown marijuana

States (and District) Allowing the Use of Medical Marijuana, December 2010

WA 1998
OR 1998
MT 2004
ND
MN
VT 2004 NH ME 1999
ID
SD
WI
NY
MA
NV 2000
WY
IA
MI 2008
PA
RI 2006
UT
NE
IL IN OH
CT
CA 1996
CO 2000
KS
MO
WV VA
DE NJ 2010
MD
AZ 2010
NM 2007
OK
AR
KY
NC
DC 2010
TN
SC
TX
MS AL GA
LA
FL

AK 1998

HI 2000

■ = state allows use

plants are permitted, which can generate thousands of joints annually. What other medicine is dispensed in such huge quantities? This will only encourage diversion of marijuana to kids.

Under the bill, you will only have to be 18 to get marijuana. Many 18-year-olds are still in high school. The average marijuana plant can produce anywhere from one to five pounds of smokable materials per year, resulting in a total harvest of between 12 and 60 pounds. Who will oversee its output and ensure that patients don't overmedicate, or that the excess production isn't diverted for recreational purposes? Massachusetts is opening a Pandora's box by traveling down this road.

Medical marijuana impacts kids. It's hard to tell kids not to smoke pot when the Legislature is telling them it is medicine. We have seen firsthand the devastation that drugs bring, not only to individuals who use them, but to their families and friends. We should not be in the position of trying to justify to young people why smoking

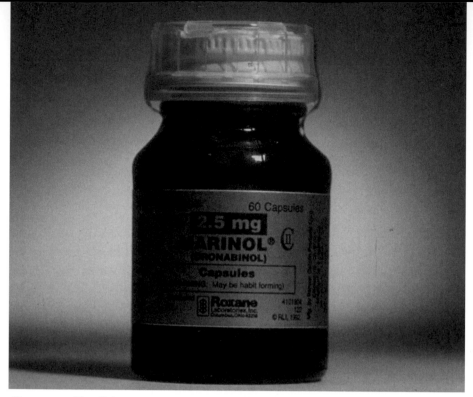

Opponents of legalizing marijuana point to synthetic THC drugs, such as Marinol, as legal alternatives for treating nausea, glaucoma, multiple sclerosis, and pain.

marijuana under certain circumstances is permissible, but is unlawful and harmful under others. A 2008 study showed that states with medical-marijuana laws constitute eight of the 10 states with the highest percentages of young people, ages 12 through 25, who have used marijuana in the past month.

Marijuana as a Medicine

Numerous effective medications—aside from marijuana—are already available to treat nausea, glaucoma, multiple sclerosis, pain and other ailments. Moreover, two FDA [US Food and Drug Administration]-approved drugs are based on cannabinoids—Marinol and Cesamet. If someone wants a marijuana-based medicine, they can get it through their doctor.

The bill permits the use of crude smoking marijuana to be used as medicine. Smoking is a poor way to deliver a drug. There's no way to calculate the dose of smoked marijuana, because there's no way to determine how much is actually inhaled. In addition, the harmful chemicals and carcinogens that are byproducts of smoking marijuana create new health problems. No other medicine is smoked because smoking is damaging to the body. Indeed, the very idea of ingesting a medicine by smoking it is counter-intuitive.

The Approval Process

Some medical organizations, such as the American College of Physicians [ACP], support research into cannabinoids. This has been used by marijuana legalization advocates as proof that these organizations support crude marijuana as medicine, but this isn't accurate. The ACP supports research into cannabinoids such as THC [tetrahydrocannabinol, the psychoactive ingredient in marijuana], but they specially state, "The ACP encourages the use of non-smoked forms of THC that have proven therapeutic value." It must be non-smoked, and it must have a proven value in the eyes of the FDA.

The medical-marijuana bill undermines our medicine approval process, carefully constructed over the past century to protect patients. There's no reason why medications derived from the cannabis plant should be exempted from the FDA process, and the FDA doesn't approve of smoking marijuana.

While we strive to be a compassionate society, there must be a balance between alleviating or managing pain and creating a system that potentially does more harm than good. The road that medical marijuana legislation is traveling is laden with potholes. There are too many unanswered questions regarding this serious public policy issue to justify its becoming law. And once the box is opened, it will be difficult to return its contents and close the lid if things don't work out.

EVALUATING THE AUTHOR'S ARGUMENTS:

In this viewpoint William T. Breault claims that over half of medical marijuana patients in California are between the ages of seventeen and thirty. How is this meant to support Breault's conclusion that medical marijuana laws are a bad idea?

Viewpoint
3

Legal Medical Marijuana Will Increase Illicit Teenage Use of Marijuana

"Legalizing medical marijuana will lead to a significant increase in marijuana use."

Mary Pat Angelini

In the following viewpoint Mary Pat Angelini laments New Jersey's approval of a medical marijuana bill and warns that the state will soon face increased illegal use of marijuana by teenagers as a result. Angelini claims that studies have shown a correlation between medical marijuana legalization and illicit teen use of marijuana. She expresses concern that the new law will allow high school students to legally possess large amounts of marijuana and calls on political leaders to prepare for the coming dangerous consequences. Angelini has been a Republican member of the New Jersey General Assembly since 2008.

AS YOU READ, CONSIDER THE FOLLOWING QUESTIONS:

1. According to Angelini, what percent of Americans who abuse illegal drugs use marijuana?
2. The author states that New Jersey will allow medical marijuana patients to possess how much marijuana per month?
3. Angelini expresses concern that politicians, instead of whom, are making decisions about medicine?

Today's teenagers seem to be growing up faster than those of previous generations. Advances in technology have catapulted the use of cell phones and computers from once being solely used as business tools into everyday necessities that define a teen's world.

While this technologically savvy generation will surely benefit from growing up accustomed to these skills, not all of the cultural advances will prove to have a positive influence on our youth. One of the most alarming differences in young adults, compared to past generations, is their drug use.

Teen Marijuana Use

According to a 2009 study performed by the National Institute on Drug Abuse, while cigarette use among the nation's teenagers has decreased, the use of marijuana has increased. The federal study on students also reported a higher use of prescription painkillers and a diminishing awareness about the risk of these illicit drugs.

A national survey by the Department of Health and Human Services showed that of the 7.1 million Americans who abuse illegal drugs, more than 60 percent abuse marijuana. With national data already showing softening attitudes and across-the-board increases for drug use, particularly marijuana, legalizing medical marijuana will lead to a significant increase in marijuana use in New Jersey.

Despite the many studies that highlight the risks of legalizing this drug, the state Legislature recently voted to legalize medical marijuana. As executive director of a nonprofit agency that provides substance abuse prevention programs to youth in Monmouth County, I know the current struggle teens have with this drug as well as the harmful path that will be paved if the drug is easier to access.

The National Institute on Drug Abuse found that medical marijuana is one of the causes of an increase in teen marijuana use. According to a recent study, 10 of the 15 states with the highest percentage of teens admitting to smoking marijuana in the last 30 days have lived in states with medical marijuana programs.

The New Jersey Law

Easier access will soon become a reality in New Jersey now that former Gov. Jon Corzine signed A-804 into law days before leaving office [January 18, 2010]. In fact, patients will only have to be 18 years of age to be prescribed medical marijuana, which is the age of many high school seniors. Further, recent amendments to the bill double the amount of marijuana that can be possessed from one ounce to two ounces per month, which means an 18-year-old high school senior can legally walk around with 240 joints.

In addition, the bill allows "for profit" medical marijuana stores to promote and sell marijuana just like the "pot shops" in California neighborhoods. These medical marijuana dispensaries have also been reported to have led to an increase in robberies and drug abuse in the surrounding areas.

A National Institute on Drug Abuse study reports that medical marijuana legalization has led to an increase in teen use in ten out of fifteen states that have legalized medicinal marijuana.

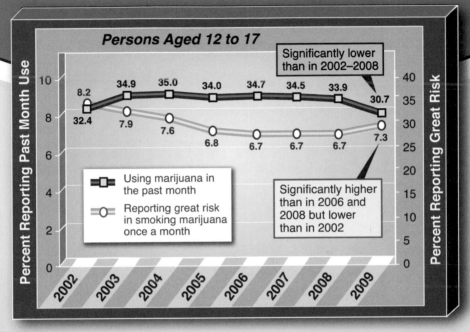

Current Use and Perceived Risk of Marijuana Use Among Youth, 2002–2009

Persons Aged 12 to 17

Percent Reporting Past Month Use

Percent Reporting Great Risk

Significantly lower than in 2002–2008

8.2 / 32.4 · 34.9 · 35.0 / 7.9 · 7.6 / 34.0 · 6.8 · 34.7 / 6.7 · 34.5 / 6.7 · 33.9 / 6.7 · 30.7 / 7.3

Using marijuana in the past month

Reporting great risk in smoking marijuana once a month

Significantly higher than in 2006 and 2008 but lower than in 2002

2002 2003 2004 2005 2006 2007 2008 2009

Taken from: ONDCP, "Marijuana Legalization: A Bad Idea," October 2010.

I have long advocated against this bill and strongly feel that legalizing medical marijuana in New Jersey is a terrible mistake. Any state considering medical marijuana should look closely at the abuse that resulted in California.

The Consequences of Legalization

In addition to all of the societal consequences, the bill would place a financial burden on the residents of New Jersey by requiring the state to employ the departments of Health and Senior Services, Agriculture, Law and Public Safety, Health and Senior Services, as well as the New Jersey State Police, to administer and monitor the program. It is also troubling that the Legislature, not trained scientists, will now decide which medicines are safe treatments for chronic diseases.

The Food and Drug Administration, which studies and approves all medicines in the United States, has made it clear that the raw marijuana plant is not medicine. Taking this authority from scientists and giving it to politicians is a gross bastardization of the process of researching and approving medicines in this country.

In the coming months, Gov. Chris Christie's choice for the commissioner of Health and Senior Services will be required to issue regulations that govern how this policy is implemented. As such, I urge Christie to direct his appointee for this important role to be mindful of the many dangers associated with this new policy. In addition, I am hopeful his administration will work to combat the increase in marijuana use among our state's young people that will likely result from this dramatic shift in New Jersey's drug policy.

> ## EVALUATING THE AUTHOR'S ARGUMENTS:
>
> In this viewpoint Mary Pat Angelini claims that the National Institute on Drug Abuse has found medical marijuana to be one of the causes of increased teen marijuana use. Name at least one objection to this finding raised by Karen O'Keefe, Mitch Earleywine, and Bruce Mirken, authors of the previous viewpoint.

Legal Medical Marijuana Does Not Increase Illicit Teenage Use of Marijuana

Karen O'Keefe, Mitch Earleywine, and Bruce Mirken

"The available evidence strongly suggests . . . that enactment of state medical marijuana laws has not increased adolescent marijuana use."

In the following viewpoint Karen O'Keefe, Mitch Earleywine, and Bruce Mirken argue that the claim that state laws legalizing medical marijuana lead to increased teen marijuana use is unfounded. The authors survey the data from several states that have laws allowing medical marijuana, concluding that the data shows that all states have experienced a decrease in teen marijuana use since enacting medical marijuana laws. O'Keefe is assistant director of state policies at the Marijuana Policy Project, an organization focused on removing criminal penalties for marijuana use; Earleywine is associate professor of psychology at the University of Albany in New York; and Mirken is the former director of communications at the Marijuana Policy Project.

In *Rhode Island*, (which passed its law in January 2006), current and lifetime youth marijuana use have decreased since the law passed. *New Mexico*, which enacted a medical marijuana law in April 2007, has not yet produced statistically valid data covering the period since its laws were passed.

The Nationwide Trends

Nationwide, teenage marijuana use has decreased in the 11 years since California enacted the country's first effective medical marijuana law. Overall, the trends in states with medical marijuana laws are more favorable than the trends nationwide. California and Washington have seen much greater drops in marijuana usage than have occurred nationwide. Overall, Nevada's, Hawaii's, and Colorado's trends are also more favorable than nationwide trends, though some individual measures are less favorable. The Youth Risk Behavior Surveillance Survey found greater declines in Maine teens' marijuana use than occurred nationally, but comparing two different surveys suggests national declines that are somewhat sharper than declines among Maine's adolescents. The drop in high schoolers' marijuana use in Vermont and Rhode Island is slightly better than the national drop. In Montana, current use has not dropped quite as quickly as the national drop, but teens' lifetime use has decreased more than the national average. Most of the trends in Oregon are slightly less favorable than nationwide trends, although teen use is still down overall.

When states consider proposals to allow the medical use of marijuana under state law, the concern often arises that such laws might "send the wrong message" and therefore cause an increase in marijuana use among young people. The available evidence strongly suggests that this hypothesis is incorrect and that enactment of

A store in California sells medical marijuana. Since California's medical marijuana law passed in 1996, the state has seen a decline in teen use of marijuana.

state medical marijuana laws has not increased adolescent marijuana use. Consequently, legislators should evaluate medical marijuana proposals based on their own merits—without regard for the speculative and unsupported assertions about the bills sending the "wrong message."

Lax Federal Enforcement of Medical Marijuana Prohibition Is a Good Idea

"Sick people in states that have legalized medicinal marijuana need not fear being prosecuted or jailed for seeking treatment recommended by their doctors."

Ventura County Star

In the following viewpoint the *Ventura County Star* argues that it was right for the federal government to respect state medical marijuana laws by having a policy of not prosecuting medical marijuana users in those states. The author explains how the federal law classifying marijuana as a schedule 1 substance has created a conflict with state laws that allow the medical use of the drug. The *Ventura County Star* says that it is outrageous that sick people who use medicine prescribed by their doctor should have to fear criminal prosecution and, thus, welcomes the change of policy. The *Ventura County Star* is a daily newspaper in Ventura County, California.

"Sane Policy at Long Last: Relief for Medicinal-Pot Users," *Ventura County Star,* March 22, 2009. www.vcstar .com. Reproduced by permission.

AS YOU READ, CONSIDER THE FOLLOWING QUESTIONS:
1. According to the author, in the past what law has superseded state law allowing the medical use of marijuana?
2. According to the author, marijuana's classification as a schedule I drug means that it may not be used for what purpose, unlike a schedule II drug?
3. What other policy regarding medical marijuana use would the author like to see changed?

Finally, there is sanity in federal policy regarding states that have legalized medicinal marijuana, including California.

Federal and State Marijuana Laws

Proposition 215—allowing the use of marijuana for medical purposes, if recommended by a physician—passed overwhelmingly in California 13 years ago. Despite that, the federal government continued to prosecute medicinal-marijuana users and dispensary groups. It has been able to do so because federal law outlawing marijuana cultivation and use supersedes state law. The conflicting laws have created a legal Catch-22 that defies logic.

Until now.

Wednesday [March 18, 2009], U.S. Attorney General Eric Holder said the U.S. Justice Department will not prosecute medicinal-marijuana dispensaries that follow the laws of the state in which they operate. Although Barack Obama indicated during his campaign that he would change the old policy, after his inauguration, the Drug Enforcement [Administration, or DEA] was still raiding medical-marijuana dispensaries in states where they were legal. Now, we presume the DEA has gotten the memo.

> **FAST FACT**
>
> In *Gonzales v. Raich* (2005) the US Supreme Court ruled that Congress's constitutional authority to regulate the interstate market in drugs extends to small, homegrown quantities of doctor-recommended marijuana in states where it is legal.

We hope to hear no more stories of sick people with cancer, eating disorders, glaucoma, AIDS and other illnesses being prosecuted for using marijuana recommended by their physicians.

The Federal Controlled Substances Act

As a result of 1970s drug-war policies, marijuana was listed as a schedule 1 drug, meaning it was deemed to have no medical use. That, despite the fact that cocaine is listed as a schedule 2 drug, available by prescription. The schedule 1 designation for marijuana remained even after a yearlong study in 1999 by the Institute of Medicine at the National Academy of Science concluded marijuana's effectiveness in treating certain ailments, including nausea and vomiting caused by chemotherapy in cancer patients.

Last year [2008], the American College of Physicians—a group of 124,000 doctors of internal medicine—called on the federal government to ease its ban on medical marijuana.

California attorney general Jerry Brown wrote that Proposition 215 did not conflict with the federal Controlled Substance Act because California did not legalize medical marijuana. Rather, the state exercised its right not to punish certain marijuana offenses, such as those in which physicians prescribe the drug to seriously ill patients.

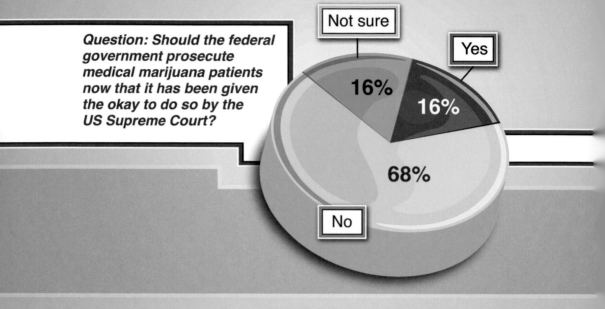

Poll on Federal Prosecution of Medical Marijuana Patients

Question: Should the federal government prosecute medical marijuana patients now that it has been given the okay to do so by the US Supreme Court?

Not sure

Yes

16%

16%

68%

No

Taken from: Mason-Dixon Poll on Medical Marijuana, Washington DC, June 2005.

State officials tried to finesse the state-federal law conflict in last year's "Guidelines for the Security and Non-Diversion of Marijuana Grown for Medical Use." In the 11-page document, California Attorney General Jerry Brown wrote: Neither Proposition 215 nor the state's 2004 Medical Marijuana Program conflict with the federal Controlled Substances Act because "in adopting these laws, California did not 'legalize' medical marijuana, but instead exercised the state's reserved powers to not punish certain marijuana offenses under state law when a physician has recommended its use to treat a serious medical condition."

Not even the U.S. Supreme Court could speak straight in its 6–3 vote in 2005 that state medical marijuana laws do not protect people from federal prosecution. Justice John Paul Stevens wrote that the court based its decision solely on the technical interstate commerce aspect of the case and not the medical-necessity defense. The court punted, saying the issue belongs before Congress.

A Welcome Policy

So, after 13 years of this ongoing dilemma, spanning the [Bill] Clinton and [George W.] Bush administrations, someone at the federal level at last says something that doesn't need legal gymnastics to grasp:

Sick people in states that have legalized medicinal marijuana need not fear being prosecuted or jailed for seeking treatment recommended by their doctors.

Now that Attorney General Holder has articulated this welcome policy, we hope transplant hospital administrators get the message and don't kick any more patients off their transplant lists just because they used medical marijuana.

Ridiculous laws can have ridiculous and tragic results.

> ## EVALUATING THE AUTHOR'S ARGUMENTS:
>
> In this viewpoint the *Ventura County Star* praises the new federal policy that will not prosecute medical marijuana users in states where it is legal. What do you think the author would say about how the federal government should treat medical marijuana users in states without legal medical marijuana? Explain your answer.

Viewpoint 6

Lax Federal Enforcement of Medical Marijuana Prohibition Is a Bad Idea

Robert Weiner

"To announce and implement a policy of broad-brush non-enforcement . . . is a dangerous policy."

In the following viewpoint Robert Weiner warns that the federal policy of lax enforcement of federal laws for the use of medical marijuana is a dangerous course of action. Weiner claims that many people using medical marijuana are not actually sick and those who are sick are being given false hope by use of marijuana. He maintains that smokable marijuana is not a safe drug and that the new policy will cause increased use along with the negative consequences. He concludes that the drug policy of the last forty years has been working well and that it should not be softened. Weiner was the White House Drug Policy Office spokesman for more than six years and communications director of the House Select Narcotics Committee for five years.

Robert Weiner, "Marijuana Laws Up in Smoke? Lax Enforcement of Medical Uses Could Be a Beginning," *Washington Times,* October 23, 2009, p. A21. Reproduced by permission.

AS YOU READ, CONSIDER THE FOLLOWING QUESTIONS:
1. Weiner draws an analogy between marijuana and what drug legalized in the 1970s to cure cancer?
2. According to the National Institute on Drug Abuse as cited by the author, what were the leading and second-leading drugs involved in car crashes?
3. The number of regular drug users in America has fallen by approximately what fraction since the 1970s, according to Weiner?

T he Justice Department had better be careful about its new lax enforcement policy for medical marijuana. The department has issued a new policy barring states attorneys from busting and prosecuting users and caregivers of so-called "medical" marijuana who act "in accordance with state law."

Here's what might actually happen: "Prescription marijuana" use may explode for healthy people.

A False Hope

Unfortunately, as many as 90 percent of purchases at clinical distribution centers are "false defenses," some law enforcement agents report—which means individuals are not really sick but simply want the pot.

Many medical experts also believe that "medical" marijuana is not as effective as other healing

> **FAST FACT**
>
> Despite the federal policy announced in 2009 to not prosecute medical marijuana patients or providers, the Drug Enforcement Administration raided several marijuana collectives in 2010.

mechanisms for many illnesses such as glaucoma, pain, or nausea for which users try it. The false hype leads to false hope. Just as laetrile was legalized in the 1970s in 27 states to cure cancer but was found to be useless apricot pits, causing the late Sen. Edward M. Kennedy to decry then in a Senate hearing the "false hope" delaying true treatment, "medical" marijuana today could be a placebo delaying far better treatments.

Medical marijuana advocates press its use for painkilling and appetite enhancement, but you might feel just as good after a shot of gin, and certainly your pain is gone with appropriate morphine or other properly tested and applied drugs. Science, not politics, must drive what is determined to be safe and effective medicine in America.

An Unsafe Drug

The medical marijuana advocates never mention the potentially better applications of THC [tetrahydrocannabinol, marijuana's psychoactive ingredient] in marijuana from suppositories, jells, aerosols or the already approved pill Marinol—they just want the high from the smoked version. After all the years of discussion, of course, science has not found that hot, smoked carcinogens in a patient's lung is the best medicine.

There is a real danger that if marijuana is made essentially a prescription drug, its abuse and usage explosion could parallel other prescription drugs over the last decade, such as OxyContin, which have tripled nationally and quintupled in many locations because of

A customer smells samples of medical marijuana at a California dispensary. Law enforcement officials say that 90 percent of clinical marijuana distribution centers—rather than serving people with medical issues—are simply selling the drug to recreational users.

"SMOKE TWO JOINTS AND CALL ME IN THE MORNING..."

"A Medical Marijuana Opinion," cartoon by Bill Schorr, Cagle Cartoons. Copyright © 2009 Bill Schorr, Cagle Cartoons, and PoliticalCartoons.com. All rights reserved. Reproduced with permission.

the ease of availability. OxyContin has become the "new heroin," and now marijuana could take its place.

Marijuana is *not* a safe drug—not only has the National Institute on Drug Abuse found that it causes dependency, but it is the second leading drug involved in car crashes, surpassed only by alcohol. The Maryland Shock Trauma Unit a few years back even found a higher rate—34 percent—of patients tested positive for marijuana than alcohol (33 percent).

A Dangerous Policy

No one wants to deny a dying cancer patient a hit of grass, if that's what he or she wants. But to announce and implement a policy of broad-brush nonenforcement when usage of medical marijuana and its distribution are so loosely controlled is a dangerous policy.

The new policy, a three-page Justice Department memo anyone can download, does not only say leave the users alone. It also says leave the "caregivers" alone if they comply with state law.

The distribution centers, which are suppliers, and the staff could well be "caregivers" who would be given the same freedoms as the patients. Because of the known voluminous fraudulent illness claims, these suppliers and staff may well in fact be just plain dealers. The Justice Department would have serious problems discerning between illicit dealers and distributors to and at clinics.

The advocates of medical marijuana say drug policy has been a failure, but the numbers say quite the reverse. While more treatment must be provided, the numbers of regular drug abusers in America has been cut sharply by almost half—from 14 percent to 8 percent—since the peak of the 1970s. Cocaine use has been cut by 70 percent. Those are real numbers from the Department of Health and Human Services.

If any other social problem such as literacy, hunger, or lack of health insurance, were cut by 40 percent or 70 percent, would we say it's a failure? Of course not. The American team effort to reduce drug abuse, including education, prevention, treatment, community coalitions, media, law enforcement, and foreign policy, actually works, and we must continue it, with improvements.

EVALUATING THE AUTHOR'S ARGUMENTS:

In this viewpoint Robert Weiner says that "no one wants to deny a dying cancer patient a hit of grass." In light of the rest of his viewpoint, do you think this indicates that Weiner believes there is room for some legal use of marijuana by the sick? Defend your answer.

Chapter 3

Should Marijuana Be Legalized?

Many controversies surround the legalization of medical marijuana, in part because it has become a big money-making industry.

Marijuana Should Be Legalized

Gary Johnson

"The common sense approach to marijuana is that we should tax it, regulate it and control it."

In the following viewpoint Gary Johnson argues that the time has come to legalize marijuana. Johnson claims that the prohibition of marijuana costs far too much money and causes too much crime. Johnson contends that legalization would help the economy by bringing in money through taxes and cutting the spending associated with prohibition and marijuana-related law enforcement costs. Johnson claims that marijuana should be taxed and regulated just like alcohol and cigarettes. He says that public support for marijuana legalization is high, having greatly expanded in recent years, supporting the idea that the time for legalization has come. Johnson is founder of the Our America Initiative, a political advocacy organization, and served as the Republican governor of New Mexico from 1995 to 2003.

AS YOU READ, CONSIDER THE FOLLOWING QUESTIONS:

1. According to Johnson, how much money do American taxpayers pay per year in law enforcement costs related to marijuana prohibition?
2. Marijuana is an industry worth how much a year, according to the author?
3. Johnson says that over the past fifteen years public support for marijuana legalization has changed in what way?

Talking points, rhetoric and political spin aside, one thing is clear: We are not winning the war on drugs. Billions of dollars are being wasted each year, countless law enforcement resources have been expended, and sadly, the result has not been a decrease in marijuana production or even a decrease in marijuana use. On the contrary, the only clear result is wasted funds and an alarming increase in crime rates.

Studies show that the prohibition of marijuana costs American taxpayers approximately $42 billion per year in law enforcement costs, as well as lost potential tax revenucs. In addition, drug cartels continue to reap huge profits due to the U.S. prohibition of marijuana—with up to 70 percent of their total profits based on marijuana sales in the United States.

American border crime is not caused by immigration. It is caused by drugs.

We learned a valuable lesson with alcohol prohibition in this country. Prohibition created black markets and violence as gangs fought to control the market. The same thing is true today. Mexican cartels reap enormous profits distributing marijuana in American cities, and the resulting violence is tragic. The nature of our current prohibition laws has forced drug disputes to be played out with guns

> ## FAST FACT
>
> In November 2010 California's Proposition 19, also known as the Marijuana Legalization Initiative, failed to garner enough votes to pass.

Do you think the use of marijuana should be made legal, or not?

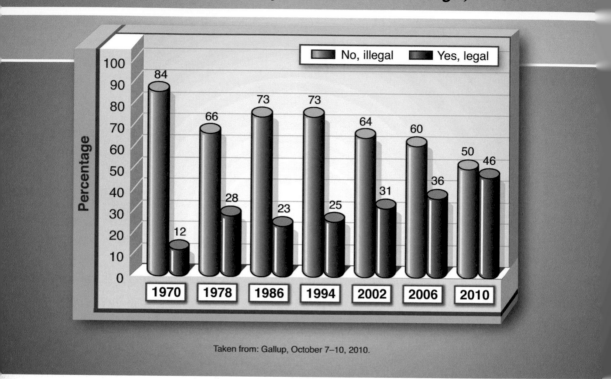

Taken from: Gallup, October 7–10, 2010.

in our streets. Simply put, if it were not for the prohibition laws in this country, the drug cartels would not be in business.

Removing the prohibition laws on marijuana would have direct significant effects on the economy. Right now, Washington is borrowing 43 cents out of every dollar being spent. Rather than wasting billions every year trying to stamp out marijuana, we should tax it. Marijuana is this country's largest cash crop, a $36 billion-a-year industry that is bigger than corn and wheat combined. This revenue we could use.

I have been a vocal advocate for the legalization of marijuana for more than 10 years, since I served as governor of New Mexico. While some may see this as a precarious political position, I see it as the only position that makes sense.

America would be a better place to live if all the resources we currently put toward criminalizing marijuana use were more wisely spent by law enforcement on protection from real crime, as opposed to victimless crime.

I am not advocating or encouraging recreational drug use, nor do I encourage the use of tobacco or alcohol recreationally. They are not healthy lifestyle choices.

But should the government really be making those kinds of choices for us? Why is there a difference being made on how we regulate marijuana and how we regulate tobacco or alcohol?

When we see government regulation and laws causing more harm than good, that is the time to change those laws. Tens of millions of American adults should have the right to live their life as they choose, provided they do no harm to anyone else. The common sense approach to marijuana is that we should tax it, regulate it and control it.

Marijuana legalization is the most effective and expedient way to reduce the exorbitant costs the United States currently spends fighting the war on drugs and the crime it creates. The ability to generate

Marijuana is the country's largest cash crop, bringing in nearly $36 billion a year. Enforcement of drug laws costs taxpayers approximately $42 billion a year.

millions in tax revenues for state governments is an additional and significant benefit. For these reasons, public opinion on the legalization of marijuana is beginning to shift.

Recent national polls have put public support for marijuana legalization at 44 percent. However, when respondents are asked to compare marijuana to alcohol and whether marijuana should be regulated and taxed by states in the same way, public support shifts even higher. Whichever poll we look at, there is a striking and consistent trend: Public support for marijuana legalization has doubled over the past 15 years.

At long last, it appears this issue is ready to be played out in the forefront of American politics. Marijuana legalization? Its time has come.

EVALUATING THE AUTHOR'S ARGUMENTS:

In this viewpoint Gary Johnson argues that marijuana should be regulated like tobacco and alcohol. What other authors in this chapter agree with Johnson on this point?

Marijuana Should Not Be Legalized

The Christian Science Monitor

> *"Why legalize a third substance that produces ill effects, when the US has such a poor record in dealing with . . . alcohol and tobacco?"*

In the following viewpoint the *Christian Science Monitor* claims that the arguments for the legalization of marijuana are flawed, and that the drug should not be legalized. The author claims that there are many dangers associated with marijuana, including health problems and dependence. Eliminating marijuana prohibition, the author argues, will not result in a lessening of drug crime and violence as proponents claim. Furthermore, the author claims that tax revenues will not offset the increased costs to society of legalizing marijuana. The author concludes by urging older adults with experience of the drug to resist the push toward legalization because of the risks to younger people. The *Christian Science Monitor* is a daily national newspaper published in print and online.

AS YOU READ, CONSIDER THE FOLLOWING QUESTIONS:
1. According to the author, the rate of dependence for marijuana users is about the same as the dependence rate for what other drug?
2. What percent of inmates in state and federal prisons are incarcerated for marijuana possession, according to the *Christian Science Monitor*?
3. Marijuana use in the Netherlands grew by what percent in the decade after 1984, according to the author?

The American movement to legalize marijuana for regular use is on a roll. Or at least its backers say it is.

The Push Toward Marijuana Legalization

They point to California Gov. Arnold Schwarzenegger, who said in early May [2009] that it's now time to debate legalizing marijuana—though he's personally against it. Indeed, a legislative push is on in his state (and several others, such as Massachusetts and Nevada) to treat this "soft" drug like alcohol—to tax and regulate its sale, and set an age restriction on buyers.

Several recent polls show stepped-up public support for legalization. This means not only lifting restrictions on use ("decriminalization"), but also on supply—production and sales. The [Barack] Obama administration, meanwhile, says the US Drug Enforcement [Administration] will no longer raid dispensaries of medical marijuana—which is illegal under federal law—in states where it is legal.

The push toward full legalization is a well-organized, Internet-savvy campaign, generously funded by a few billionaires, including [noted liberal financier and philanthropist] George Soros. It's built on a decades-long, step-by-step effort in the states. Thirteen states have so far decriminalized marijuana use (generally, the punishment covers small amounts and involves a fine). And 13 states now allow for medical marijuana.

Paul Armentano, deputy director of the National Organization for the Reform of Marijuana Laws (NORML), recently told a *Monitor* reporter that three reasons account for the fresh momentum toward legalization: 1) the weak economy, which is forcing states to look for new revenue; 2) public concern over the violent drug war in Mexico; and 3) more experience with marijuana itself.

If there is to be a debate, let's look at these reasons, starting with experience with marijuana.

The Harms of Marijuana Use

Supporters of legalization often claim that no one has died of a pot overdose, and that it has beneficial effects in alleviating suffering from certain diseases.

True, marijuana cannot directly kill its user in the way that alcohol or a drug like heroin can. And activists claim that it may ease symptoms for certain patients—though it has not been endorsed by the major medical associations representing those patients, and the Food and Drug Administration disputes its value.

Rosalie Pacula, codirector of the Rand Drug Policy Research Center, poses this question: "If pot is relatively harmless, why are we seeing more than 100,000 hospitalizations a year" for marijuana use?

Emergency-room admissions where marijuana is the primary substance involved increased by 164 percent from 1995 to 2002—faster than for other drugs, according to the Drug Abuse Warning Network.

> **FAST FACT**
>
> Office of National Drug Control Policy director R. Gil Kerlikowske announced on October 23, 2009, that marijuana legalization was a nonstarter—having no chance of being successful—in the Barack Obama administration.

Research results over the past decade link frequent marijuana use to several serious mental health problems, with youth particularly at risk. And the British Lung Foundation finds that smoking three to four joints is the equivalent or 20 tobacco cigarettes.

While marijuana is not addictive in the way that a drug like crack-cocaine is, heavy use can lead to dependence—defined by the same criteria as for other drugs. About half of those who use pot daily

Heavy use of marijuana can lead to dependence. About half of those who use marijuana daily develop some kind of dependence.

become dependent for some period of time, writes Kevin Sabet, in the 2006 book, *Pot Politics*—and 1 in 10 people in the US who have ever used marijuana become dependent at some time (about the same rate as alcohol). Dr. Sabet was a drug policy adviser in the past two presidential administrations.

He adds that physicians in Britain and the Netherlands—both countries that have experience with relaxed marijuana laws—are seeing withdrawal symptoms among heavy marijuana users that are similar to those of cocaine and heroin addicts. This has been confirmed in the lab with monkeys.

Today's marijuana is also much more potent than in the hippie days of yesteryear. But that doesn't change what's always been known about even casual use of this drug: It distorts perception, reduces motor skills, and affects alertness. When combined with alcohol (not unusual), or even alone, it worsens the risk of traffic accidents.

Marijuana's Role in Crime and Violence

NORML likes to point out that marijuana accounts for the majority of illicit drug traffic from Mexico. End the illicit trafficking, and you end the violence. But that volume gives a false impression of marijuana's role in crime and violence, says Jonathan Caulkins, a professor at Carnegie Mellon and a drug-policy adviser in the US and Australia.

It's the dollars that count, and the big earners—cocaine, methamphetamine, heroin—play a much larger role in crime and violence. In recent years, Mexico has become a major cocaine route to the US. That's what's fanning the violence, according to Dr. Caulkins, so legalizing marijuana is unlikely to quiet Mexico's drug war.

Neither are America's prisons stuffed with users who happened to get caught with a few joints (if that were the case, a huge percentage of America's college students—an easy target—would be behind bars). Yes, there are upward of 700,000 arrests on marijuana charges each year, but that includes repeat arrests, and most of those apprehended don't go to jail. Those who do are usually large-scale offenders.

Only 0.7 percent of inmates in state and federal prisons are in for marijuana possession (0.3 percent counting first-time offenders only, according to a 2002 US Justice Department survey). In federal prisons, the median amount of marijuana for those convicted of possession is 115 pounds—156,000 marijuana cigarettes.

The Costs of Legalizing Marijuana

The California legalization bill [that failed to pass in 2010] proposes a $50/ounce tax on marijuana. The aim is to keep pot as close to the black-market price as possible while still generating an estimated $1.3 billion in income for this deficit-challenged state.

But the black market can easily undercut a $50 tax and shrink that expected revenue stream. Just look at the huge trade in illegal cigarettes in Canada to see how taxing can spur a black market (about 30 percent of tobacco bought in Canada is illegal).

A government could attempt to eliminate the black market altogether by making marijuana incredibly cheap (Dr. Pacula at the RAND [Corporation] says today's black market price is about four times what it would be if pot were completely legalized). But then use would skyrocket and teens (though barred) could buy it with their lunch money.

Indeed, legalizing marijuana is bound to increase use simply because of availability. Legalization advocates say "not so" and point to the Netherlands and its legal marijuana "coffee shops." Indeed, after the Dutch de facto legalized the drug in 1976, use stayed about the same for adults and youth. But it took off after 1984, growing by 300 percent over the next decade or so. Experts attribute this to commercialization (sound like alcohol?), and also society's view of the drug as normal—which took a while to set in.

Now the Dutch are finding that normalization has its costs—increased dependence, more dealers of harder drugs, and a flood of rowdy "drug tourists" from other countries. The Dutch "example" should be renamed the Dutch "warning."

As America has learned with alcohol, taxes don't begin to cover the costs to society of destroyed families, lost productivity, and ruined lives—and regulators still have not succeeded in keeping alcohol from underage drinkers.

No one has figured out what the exact social costs of legalizing marijuana would be. But ephemeral taxes won't cover them—nor should society want to encourage easier access to a drug that can lead to dependency, has health risks, and reduces alertness, to name just a few of its negative outcomes.

Why legalize a third substance that produces ill effects, when the US has such a poor record in dealing with the two big "licits"—alcohol and tobacco?

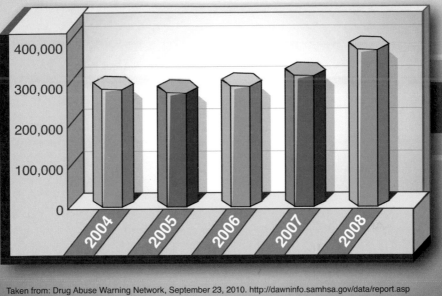

National Estimates of Marijuana-Related Emergency Department Visits, 2004–2008

Taken from: Drug Abuse Warning Network, September 23, 2010. http://dawninfo.samhsa.gov/data/report.asp ?f-Nation/All/Nation_2008_All_ED_Visits_by_Drug.

The Importance of Disapproval

Legalization backers say the country is at a tipping point, ready to make the final big leap. They hope that a new generation of politicians that has had experience with marijuana will be friendly to their cause.

But this new generation is also made up of parents. Do parents really want marijuana to become a normal part of society—and an expectation for their children?

Maybe parents thought they left peer pressure behind when they graduated from high school. But the push to legalize marijuana is like the peer pressure of the schoolyard. The arguments are perhaps timely, but they don't stand up, and parents must now stand up to them.

They must let lawmakers know that legalization is not OK, and they must carry this message to their children, too. Disapproval, along with information on risk, are the most important factors in discouraging marijuana and cocaine use among high school seniors, according to the University of Michigan's "Monitoring the Future" project on substance abuse.

Parents must make clear that marijuana is not a harmless drug—even if they personally may have emerged unscathed.

And they need to teach the life lesson that marijuana does not really solve personal challenges, be they stress, relationships, or discouragement.

In the same way, a search for joy and satisfaction in a drug is misplaced.

The far greater and lasting attraction is in a life rooted in moral and spiritual values—not in a haze, a daze, or a munchie-craze.

Today's youth are tomorrow's world problem solvers—and the ones most likely to be affected if marijuana is legalized. Future generations need to be clear thinkers. For their sakes, those who oppose legalizing marijuana must become vocal, well-funded, and mainstream—before it's too late.

EVALUATING THE AUTHOR'S ARGUMENTS:

In this viewpoint the *Christian Science Monitor* attempts to refute many of the arguments in favor of legalization. Name one argument in favor of legalization raised by another author in this chapter that the *Christian Science Monitor* attempts to refute.

Legalizing Marijuana Would Have Many Positive Effects

Tom Barnidge

"Legalization represents a major reversal in policy, but that doesn't make it bad."

In the following viewpoint Tom Barnidge claims that there are benefits to legalizing marijuana. Barnidge claims that many current and former law enforcement officials support legalizing marijuana. He says this is because they have seen firsthand the failure of the war on drugs. Among the benefits he cites are better use of law enforcement resources and increased state revenues. Furthermore, he claims that in the long run the legalization of marijuana will make the drug appear boring, leading to a decline in use, which he claims has occurred in the Netherlands. Barnidge is a columnist for the *Contra Costa Times*, a daily newspaper in Walnut Creek, California.

AS YOU READ, CONSIDER THE FOLLOWING QUESTIONS:

1. According to Barnidge, the war on drugs that began in 1971 has lasted how long?
2. According to the author, what percent of the US population was addicted to drugs in 1914, 1971, and 2006, respectively?
3. State sales tax revenues from legalization of marijuana are estimated to amount to how much, according to Barnidge?

When the Assembly's Public Safety Committee voted 12 days ago to approve the legalization and regulation of marijuana, knee-jerk reactions were sure to follow.

This was only a first step toward legislation, but San Mateo police Chief Susan Manheimer quickly described the looming possibility as "mind-boggling."

John Lovell, speaking for the California Peace Officers Association, said it was "the last thing our society needs."

It wasn't hard to envision lawmen up and down the state nodding in agreement.

The viewpoint is understandable. It is part of the internal wiring of police agencies. The War on Drugs declared by President Nixon in 1971 has spanned four decades and seven administrations.

The thing is, it has failed. A far better idea is to legalize and regulate marijuana sales.

> **FAST FACT**
>
> On October 27, 1970, the Richard Nixon administration implemented the Comprehensive Drug Abuse Prevention and Control Act of 1970, which includes the Controlled Substances Act.

There are at least 1,500 current and former law enforcement professionals who agree. They are members of LEAP (Law Enforcement Against Prohibition), who base their opinions on years of experience.

Jack Cole, co-founder of the 8-year-old organization, is a retired New Jersey State Police lieutenant who served 12 of his 26 years on the job as an undercover narcotics cop. He describes the War on Drugs as "not only a dismal failure but a terribly destructive policy."

Norm Stamper, former Seattle police chief, used to kick in drug dealers' doors early in his 34-year career. His opinion: "It has cost the national treasury obscene amounts of money. And for what?"

James Gray, an Orange County Superior Court Judge for 20 years, remembers sentencing one dealer after another to no perceptible end. "The closer you get to the issue," he said, "the more you see we couldn't do worse if we tried."

They liken the ban on recreational drugs to Prohibition, when the government's ill-fated attempt to end the sale of liquor created a lucrative industry for criminals. Sound familiar?

LEAP has packaged its argument in a convincing 12-minute video, (http://www.leap.cc/cms/index/pp7name-Content&ptd-28) in which Cole explains that an estimated 1.3 percent of the U.S. population was addicted to drugs when the Harrison Act, a national anti-drug law, was enacted in 1914.

And 1.3 percent was believed to be addicted when the War on Drugs was unveiled. And 1.3 percent was addicted when a study was conducted in 2006.

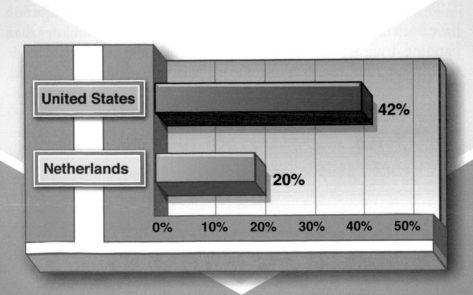

Lifetime Marijuana Use

United States: 42%
Netherlands: 20%

Taken from: Louisa Degenhardt et al., "Toward a Global View of Alcohol, Tobacco, Cannabis, and Cocaine Use: Findings from the WHO World Mental Health Surveys," *PLoS Medicine*, July 2008. Table 2.

Legalizing marijuana would not ensure that serious drug-related problems, such as violence and street gang activity, would disappear.

aggressive marketing worthwhile for sellers. Addiction is simply the price of doing business.

Would marijuana use rise in a legal market for the drug? Admittedly, marijuana is not very difficult to obtain currently, but a legal market would make getting the drug that much easier. Tobacco and alcohol are used regularly by 30% and 65% of the population, respectively, while all illegal drugs combined are used by about 6% of Americans. In the Netherlands, where marijuana is de facto legalized, lifetime use "increased consistently and sharply" after this policy shift triggered commercialization, tripling among young adults, according to data analysis from the Rand Corp. We might expect a similar or worse result here in America's ad-driven culture.

The Costs of Marijuana Arrests

An honest debate on marijuana policy also carefully considers the costs of our current approach. Arrest rates for marijuana are relatively high, reaching about 800,000 last year. Though these numbers are technically recorded under the category of "possession," the story that is seldom told is that hardly any of these possession arrests result in jail time (that is why former New York City Mayor Rudolph Giuliani made headlines when he aggressively arrested public marijuana users and detained them for 12 to 24 hours in the 1990s).

One of the most astute minds in the field of drug policy, Carnegie Mellon's Jonathan Caulkins, formerly the co-director of Rand's drug policy research center, found that more than 85% of people in prison for all drug-law violations were clearly involved in drug distribution, and that the records of most of the remaining prisoners had at least some suggestion of distribution involvement (many prisoners plea down from more serious charges to possession in exchange for information about the drug trade). Only about half a percent of the total prison population was there for marijuana possession, he found. He noted that this figure was consistent with other mainstream estimates but not with estimates from the Marijuana Policy Project (a legalization interest group), which, according to Caulkins, "naively . . . assumes that all inmates convicted of possession were not involved in trafficking."

> **FAST FACT**
>
> According to 2009 testimony by the Rand Corporation before the California State Assembly Public Safety Committee, legalizing marijuana would cause the price of marijuana to fall by more than 50 percent.

Caulkins concluded that "an implication of the new figure is that marijuana decriminalization would have almost no impact on prison populations." This is not meant to imply that marijuana arrests do not have costs, but rather, that these concerns have been highly exaggerated.

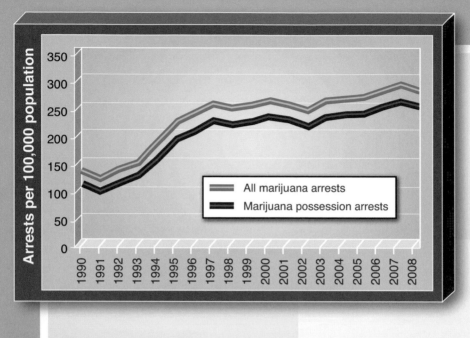

Marijuana Arrests in the United States, 1990–2008

Taken from: Beau Kilmer et al., "Altered State? Assessing How Marijuana Legalization in California Could Influence Marijuana Consumption and Public Budgts," Rand Corporation, 2010.

An Unrealistic Option

Finally, legalizing marijuana would in no way ensure that the most vicious drug-related problems—violence, economic-related crime, street gang activity—would disappear. Most of those problems stem from the cocaine, heroin and methamphetamine markets. Marijuana's share of the black market is modest (the cocaine market is three times larger), and the money that is spent on the drug is spread over so many users and distributors that few are working with amounts that motivate or encourage high levels of crime.

Moving beyond the simplistic and unrealistic option of legalization, what can we do to reduce marijuana use and the costly harms it brings? Increasing the ferocity of enforcement isn't the answer, but increasing its potential for effectiveness through deterrent methods might be. Programs like Project HOPE in Hawaii, which perform regular, random drug testing on probationers and others and implement reliable, swift (but short) sanctions for positive screens, have shown remarkable success. Innovative solutions, grounded in sound research on prevention, treatment and enforcement, present the shortest route out of marijuana-related costs. But an open market for the stuff? That doesn't pass the giggle test.

EVALUATING THE AUTHOR'S ARGUMENTS:

In this viewpoint Kevin A. Sabet uses a fact about the Netherlands' experience with marijuana to argue against legalization, whereas Tom Barnidge—author of the previous viewpoint—uses a different fact about the country's experience in an argument favoring legalization. Looking at these facts together, whose point of view do you think is better supported by these facts? Explain.

Marijuana Prohibition Is Working Well

Robert L. DuPont

"The current . . . drug policies of the United States are working reasonably well and they have contributed to reductions in the rate of marijuana use in our nation."

In the following viewpoint Robert L. DuPont argues that the prohibition on marijuana is working well and that supporters of legalization fail to take into account many positive features of the current system. DuPont claims that those in prison often get treatment for their addiction to marijuana. If legalized, he says, addiction would increase without the available avenues or funds for adequate treatment. DuPont contends that the increased use of marijuana from legalization would also increase public-safety dangers on the roads and elsewhere. DuPont concludes that the current policies aimed at curbing marijuana use, including its status as an illegal drug, need to be continued. DuPont is a fellow of the American Society of Addiction Medicine, who served as the director of the National Institute on Drug Abuse from 1973 to 1978, and was the White House drug czar from 1973 to 1977 under presidents Richard Nixon and Gerald Ford.

C ontrary to the beliefs of those who advocate the legalization of marijuana, the current balanced, restrictive, and bipartisan drug policies of the United States are working reasonably well and they have contributed to reductions in the rate of marijuana use in our nation.

The rate of current, past 30-day use of marijuana by Americans aged 12 and older in 1979 was 13.2 percent. In 2008 that figure stood at 6.1 percent. This 54-percent reduction in marijuana use over that 29-year period is a major public health triumph, not a failure.

The Benefit of Treatment

Marijuana is the most commonly abused illegal drug in the U.S. and around the world. Those who support its legalization, for medical or for general use, fail to recognize that the greatest costs of marijuana are not related to its prohibition; they are the costs resulting from marijuana use itself.

There is a common misconception that the principal costs of marijuana use are those related to the criminal justice system. This is a false premise. [J.P.] Caulkins & [E.L.] Sevigny found that the percentage of people in prison for marijuana use is less than one half of one percent (0.1–0.2 percent).

An encounter with the criminal justice system through apprehension for a drug-related crime frequently can benefit the offender because the criminal justice system is often a path to treatment.

More than a third, 37 percent, of treatment admissions reported in the Treatment Episode Data Set, TEDS, collected from state-funded programs were referred through the criminal justice system.

Marijuana was an identified drug of abuse for 57 percent of the individuals referred to treatment from the criminal justice system. The future of drug policy is not a choice between using the criminal justice system or treatment. The more appropriate goal is to get these two systems to work together more effectively to improve both public safety and public health.

An Analogy with Gambling

In the discussion of legalizing marijuana, a useful analogy can be made to gambling. [R.J.] MacCoun & [P.] Reuter conclude that making the government a beneficiary of legal gambling has encouraged the government to promote gambling, overlooking it as a problem behavior. They point out that "the moral debasement of state government is a phenomenon that only a few academics and preachers bemoan."

Legalized gambling has not reduced illegal gambling in the United States; rather, it has increased it. This is particularly evident in sports gambling, most of which is illegal. Legal gambling is taxed and regulated and illegal gambling is not. Legal gambling sets the stage for illegal gambling just the way legal marijuana would set the stage for illegal marijuana trafficking.

The gambling precedent suggests strongly that illegal drug suppliers would thrive by selling more potent marijuana products outside of the legal channels that would be taxed and otherwise restricted. If marijuana were legalized, the only way to eliminate its illegal trade, which is modest in comparison to that of cocaine, would be to sell marijuana untaxed and unregulated to any willing buyer.

The Problem of Addiction

Marijuana is currently the leading cause of substance dependence other than alcohol in the U.S. In 2008, marijuana use accounted for

"Wish I could!"

"Keep off the grass: 'Wish I could,'" cartoon by Ray Jelliffe, www.CartoonStock.com. Copyright © by Ray Jelliffe. Reproduction rights obtainable from www.CartoonStock.com.

4.2 million of the 7 million people aged 12 or older classified with dependence on or abuse of an illicit drug. This means that about two thirds of Americans suffering from any substance use disorder are suffering from marijuana abuse or marijuana dependence.

If the U.S. were to legalize marijuana, the number of marijuana users would increase. Today there are 15.2 million current marijuana users in comparison to 129 million alcohol users and 70.9 million tobacco users. Though the number of marijuana users might not quickly climb to the current numbers for alcohol and tobacco, if marijuana was legalized, the increase in users would be both large and rapid with subsequent increases in addiction.

Important lessons can be learned from these two widely-used legal drugs. While both alcohol and tobacco are taxed and regulated, the tax benefits to the public are vastly overshadowed by the adverse consequences of their use.

Alcohol-related costs total over $185 billion while federal and states collected an estimated $14.5 billion in tax revenue; similarly, tobacco use costs over $200 billion but only $25 billion is collected in taxes. These figures show that the costs of legal alcohol are more than 12 times the total tax revenue collected, and that the costs of legal tobacco are about 8 times the tax revenue collected. This is an economically disastrous tradeoff.

The Harms of Marijuana Legalization

The costs of legalizing marijuana would not only be financial. New marijuana users would not be limited to adults if marijuana were legalized, just as regulations on alcohol and tobacco do not prevent use by youth. Rapidly accumulating new research shows that marijuana use is associated with increases in a range of serious mental and physical problems. Lack of public understanding on this relationship is undermining prevention efforts and adversely affecting the nation's youth and their families.

Drug-impaired driving will also increase if marijuana is legalized. Marijuana is already a significant causal factor in highway crashes, injuries and deaths. In a recent national roadside survey of weekend nighttime drivers, 8.6 percent tested positive for marijuana or its metabolites, nearly four times the percentage of drivers with a blood alcohol concentration (BAC) of .08 g/dL (2.2 percent).

In another study of seriously injured drivers admitted to a Level-1 shock trauma center, more than a quarter of all drivers (26.9 percent) tested positive for marijuana. In a study of fatally injured drivers in Washington State, 12.7 percent tested positive for marijuana. These studies demonstrate the high prevalence of drugged driving as a result of marijuana use.

Many people who want to legalize marijuana are passionate about their perception of the alleged failures of policies aimed at reducing marijuana use but those legalization proponents seldom—if ever—describe their own plan for taxing and regulating marijuana as a legal drug. There is a reason for this imbalance; they cannot come up with a credible plan for legalization that could deliver on their exaggerated claims for this new policy.

The Need to Reduce Marijuana Use

Future drug policies must be smarter and more effective in curbing the demand for illegal drugs including marijuana. Smarter-drug prevention policies should start by reducing illegal drug use among the 5 million criminal offenders who are on parole and probation in the U.S. They are among the nation's heaviest and most problem-generating illegal drug users.

Monitoring programs that are linked to swift and certain, but not severe, consequences for any drug use have demonstrated outstanding results including lower recidivism and lower rates of incarceration. New policies to curb drugged driving will not only make our roads and highways safer and provide an important new path to treatment, but they will also reduce illegal drug use.

Reducing marijuana use is essential to improving the nation's health, education, and productivity. New policies can greatly improve current performance of prevention strategies which, far from failing, has protected millions of people from the many adverse effects of marijuana use.

Critics point to the fact that legalized gambling has not reduced illegal gambling in the United States; they claim that legalizing marijuana would only encourage more illegal trafficking.

Since legalization of marijuana for medical or general use would increase marijuana use rather than reduce it and would lead to increased rates of addiction to marijuana among youth and adults, legalizing marijuana is not a smart public health or public safety strategy for any state or for our nation.

EVALUATING THE AUTHOR'S ARGUMENTS:

In this viewpoint Robert L. DuPont draws an analogy with gambling to support his view that marijuana should remain illegal. How might John McKay, author of the following viewpoint, use that same analogy in support of marijuana legalization?

Viewpoint

6

Marijuana Prohibition Is a Poor Policy That Needs to End

John McKay

"Our marijuana policy is dangerous and wrong and should be changed through the legislative process to better protect the public safety."

In the following viewpoint John McKay argues that current marijuana policy is ineffective and dangerous. McKay believes that criminal prohibition of marijuana has failed, evidenced in part by the large number of regular marijuana users. He claims that law enforcement cannot implement the current prohibition, especially in light of legal medical marijuana in many states. McKay suggests a change in policy that focuses on educating about the risks of marijuana and allowing legal consumption by adults. He concludes that changing policy on marijuana will allow law enforcement to focus on enforcing the prohibition of truly dangerous drugs. McKay is a professor of law at Seattle University School of Law and a former US attorney for western Washington.

The Seattle Times, September 3, 2010, for "Marijuana's True Potency and Why the Law Should Change," by John McKay. Reproduced by permission of the author.

AS YOU READ, CONSIDER THE FOLLOWING QUESTIONS:
  1. According to McKay, marijuana is listed by the US government in the same category as what other illegal drug?
  2. What conflict of laws does the author claim is problematic with current marijuana policy?
  3. McKay suggests maintaining criminal penalties for marijuana use by whom?

I don't smoke pot. And I pretty much think people who do are idiots.

Current Marijuana Policy

This certainly includes Marc Emery, the self-styled "Prince of Pot" from Canada whom I indicted in 2005 for peddling marijuana seeds to every man, woman and child with an envelope and a stamp. Emery recently pleaded guilty and will be sentenced this month in Seattle, where he faces five years in federal prison. [He was sentenced to five years on September 10, 2010.] If changing U.S. marijuana policy was ever Emery's goal, the best that can be said is that he took the wrong path.

As Emery's prosecutor and a former federal law-enforcement official, however, I'm not afraid to say out loud what most of my former colleagues know is true: Our marijuana policy is dangerous and wrong and should be changed through the legislative process to better protect the public safety.

Congress has failed to recognize what many already know about our policy of criminal prohibition of marijuana—it has utterly failed. Listed by the U.S. government as a "Schedule One" drug alongside heroin, the demand for marijuana in this country for decades has outpaced the ability of law enforcement to eliminate it. Perhaps this is because millions of Americans smoke pot regularly and international drug cartels, violent gangs and street pushers work hard to reap the profits.

Law-enforcement agencies are simply not capable of interdicting all of this pot and despite some successes have not succeeded in thwarting criminals who traffic and sell marijuana. Brave agents and cops continue to risk their lives in a futile attempt to enforce misguided laws that do not match the realities of our society.

The Harms of the Current Policy

These same agents and cops, along with prosecutors, judges and jailers, know we can't win by arresting all those involved in the massive importation, growth or distribution of marijuana, nor by locking up all the pot smokers. While many have argued the policy is unjust, few have addressed the dangerously potent black market the policy itself has created for exploitation by Mexican and other international drug cartels and gangs. With the proceeds from the U.S. marijuana black market, these criminals distribute dangerous drugs and kill each other (too often along with innocent bystanders) with American-purchased guns.

Our wrongheaded policy on marijuana has also failed to address the true health threat posed by its use. While I suspect nothing good can come to anyone from the chronic ingestion of marijuana smoke, its addictive quality and health risk pale in comparison with other

Marc Emery (left), Canada's self-described "Prince of Pot," was sentenced to five years in federal prison for distributing marijuana seeds through the mail to hundreds of people.

banned drugs such as heroin, cocaine or meth. Informed adult choice, albeit a bad one, may well be preferable to the legal and policy meltdown we have long been suffering over marijuana.

Not only does our policy directly threaten our public safety and rest upon false medical assumptions, but our national laws are now in direct and irreconcilable conflict with state laws, including Washington state. So called "medical" marijuana reaches precious few patients and backdoor potheads mock legitimate medical use by glaucoma and chemotherapy patients. State laws are trumped by federal laws that recognize no such thing as "medicinal" or "personal" use and are no defense to arrests by federal agents and prosecution in federal courts.

A Change in Policy

So the policy is wrong, the law has failed, the public is endangered, no one in law enforcement is talking about it and precious few policymakers will honestly face the soft-on-crime sound bite in their next elections. What should be done?

- First, we need to honestly and courageously examine the true public-safety danger posed by criminalizing a drug used by millions and millions of Americans who ignore the law. Marijuana prohibition has failed—it's time for a new policy crafted by informed policymakers with the help of those in law enforcement who have risked their lives battling pot-purveying drug cartels and gangs.
- Second, let's talk about marijuana policy responsibly and with an eye toward sound science, not myth. We can start by acknowledging that our 1930s-era marijuana prohibition was overkill from the beginning and should be decoupled from any debate about "legalizing drugs." We should study and disclose the findings of

the real health risks of prolonged use, including its influence and effect on juveniles.

- Third, we should give serious consideration to heavy regulation and taxation of the marijuana industry (an industry that is very real and dangerously underground). We should limit pot's content of the active ingredient THC (tetrahydrocannabinol), regulate its sale to adults who are dumb enough to want it and maintain criminal penalties for sales, possession or use by minors, drivers and boaters.

Federal criminal law should give way to regulation, while prohibiting interstate violation of federal laws consistent with this approach. In short, policymakers should strive for a regulatory and criminal scheme like the one guarding that other commodity that failed miserably at prohibition, alcohol.

As my law-enforcement colleagues know well from chasing bootleggers and mobsters, this new regulatory and criminal approach will still require many years of intensive investigation and enforcement before

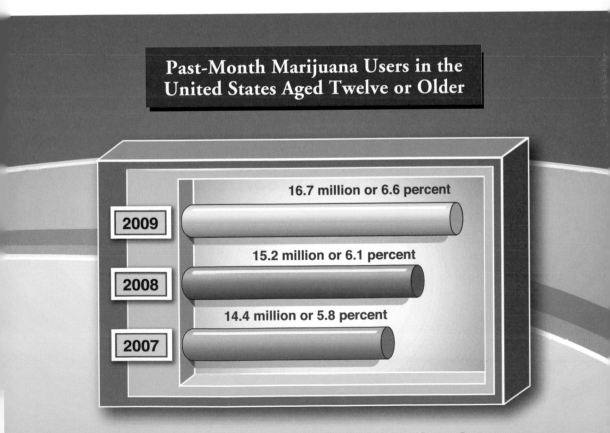

Past-Month Marijuana Users in the United States Aged Twelve or Older

16.7 million or 6.6 percent

2009

15.2 million or 6.1 percent

2008

14.4 million or 5.8 percent

2007

Taken from: Substance Abuse and Mental Health Administration, 2009 National Survey on Drug Use and Health. http://oas.samhsa.gov/nsduh.htm.

organized criminal elements are driven from the vast marijuana market. DEA [Drug Enforcement Administration] and its law-enforcement partners must therefore remain well equipped and staffed to accomplish this task: to protect our families from truly dangerous drugs and to drive drug cartels, gangs and dope dealers from our society.

EVALUATING THE AUTHOR'S ARGUMENTS:

In this viewpoint John McKay suggests changing current marijuana policy. Which authors in this chapter would agree with McKay? Which would disagree? Explain.

Facts About Marijuana

Cannabis

- Marijuana comes from the *Cannabis sativa* plant or the *Cannabis indica* plant. The dried flowers, stems, seeds, and leaves are smoked, vaporized, or eaten.
- Humans have cultivated cannabis plants throughout recorded history for use as fiber, oil, food, and a drug.
- The main psychoactive ingredient in cannabis plants that is sought in marijuana use is tetrahydrocannabinol, or THC.

Effects of Marijuana

- THC acts on cannabinoid receptors in the brain. Cannabinoid receptors are found in parts of the brain that influence pleasure, memory, thinking, concentrating, time perception, and coordinated movement.
- Marijuana intoxication can cause distorted perceptions, impaired coordination, difficulty thinking, and problems with memory.
- Marijuana increases the heart rate by 20 to 100 percent after smoking.
- Marijuana smoke contains numerous substances, including carcinogens (cancer-causing substances).
- The research regarding marijuana's long-term effects on the brain has yielded inconclusive results.

Medical Marijuana

- Marijuana can be smoked, vaporized, or eaten in order to utilize THC for its medicinal properties. Medical marijuana is used for a wide variety of conditions, including nausea, vomiting, insomnia, glaucoma, symptoms of multiple sclerosis, and other conditions, though its use as medicine continues to be controversial.
- Synthetic THC, dronabinol, has been developed for medicinal use, and is available by prescription from a doctor in the United States under the brand name Marinol. Dronabinol is used to treat nausea and vomiting caused by chemotherapy, and loss of appetite and

weight loss in people who have acquired immunodeficiency syndrome (AIDS).

- Nabilone, a synthetic cannabinoid that mimics THC, is available by prescription from a doctor in the United States under the brand name Cesamet. Nabilone is also used to treat nausea and vomiting in chemotherapy patients.
- Sativex is a mouth spray developed from cannabis plant material. Sativex is available in Canada and parts of Europe, used primarily for multiple sclerosis and pain. As of January 2011, Sativex is undergoing testing for approval in the United States.

Legal Status of Marijuana in the United States
- Marijuana is classified as a schedule I drug by the US government, meaning it is classified as having a high potential for abuse and no currently accepted medical use in treatment in the United States.
- As of January 2011, fifteen states—Alaska, Arizona, California, Colorado, Hawaii, Maine, Michigan, Montana, Nevada, New Jersey, New Mexico, Oregon, Rhode Island, Vermont, Washington—and the District of Columbia have passed legislation that decriminalizes the use of medical marijuana.
- Although state laws allowing medical marijuana-exempt patients and their prescribing physicians from prosecution for violating state laws, the state laws do not protect them from federal criminal prosecution for production, distribution, and possession.

Marijuana Use in the United States
According to the Monitoring the Future Study on Adolescent Drug Use in 2009:

- Marijuana has been the most commonly used illicit drug in the United States for the past thirty-five years.
- Marijuana use during the previous year peaked among 12th graders in 1979 at 51 percent. It bottomed out at 22 percent in 1992. By 2009 the past-year use of 12th graders rose to 33 percent.
- Among 12th graders polled in 2009, 42 percent had used marijuana at least once, 21 percent had used marijuana in the last month, and 5 percent said they used marijuana daily.
- Among 8th graders polled in 2009, 16 percent had used marijuana at least once, 12 percent had used marijuana within the last year, 7

percent had used it within the last month, and 1 percent said they used marijuana daily.

- In 2009, 40 percent of 8th graders, 69 percent of 10th graders, and 81 percent of 12th graders reported that marijuana was fairly easy or very easy to get.
- Among 18-year-olds polled in 2009, 19 percent said that they perceived people to be risking harm to themselves if they tried marijuana once or twice, 27 percent said people were risking harm by smoking marijuana occasionally, and 52 percent said that people were risking harm by smoking marijuana regularly. Twenty years prior, in 1989, the perception of harm among 18-year-olds was at 24 percent, 37 percent, and 78 percent, respectively.
- Among 18-year-olds questioned in 2009, 80 percent disapproved of adults who smoke marijuana regularly, compared with 90 percent who thought the same in 1989.

Organizations to Contact

American Alliance for Medical Cannabis (AAMC)
44500 Tide Ave., Arch Cape, OR 97102
(503) 436-1882
e-mail: contact@letfreedomgrow.com
website: www.letfreedomgrow.com

AAMC is dedicated to bringing patients, caregivers, and volunteers the facts they need to make informed decisions about medical marijuana. AAMC advocates for the rights of medical marijuana patients through education and interaction with government representatives. AAMC provides literature available at its website on the common medical uses of marijuana.

American Civil Liberties Union (ACLU)
125 Broad St., 18th Fl., New York, NY 10004
(212) 549-2500
e-mail: aclu@aclu.org
website: www.aclu.org

The ACLU is a national organization that works to defend Americans' civil rights guaranteed by the US Constitution by providing legal defense, research, and education. The ACLU opposes the criminal prohibition of marijuana and the civil liberties violations that result from it. The ACLU Drug Law Reform Project engages in campaigns and submits briefs in relevant law cases, with literature about these campaigns and text of the briefs available at the ACLU website.

American Council for Drug Education (ACDE)
164 W. Seventy-Fourth St., New York, NY 10023
(800) 488-3784
fax: (212) 595-2553
e-mail: acde@phoenixhouse.org
website: www.acde.org

ACDE seeks to diminish substance abuse. It creates accessible materials on the most current scientific research to those seeking accurate, compelling information on drugs. ACDE has resources about drug and alcohol abuse for parents, youth, educators, prevention professionals, employers, health care professionals, and other concerned community members, including fact sheets on numerous substances. ACDE is an affiliate of Phoenix House Foundation, the largest private nonprofit drug abuse service agency in the country.

Americans for Safe Access (ASA)
1322 Webster St., Ste. 402, Oakland, CA 94612
(510) 251-1856
fax: (510) 251-2036
e-mail: info@safeaccessnow.org
website: www.safeaccessnow.org

ASA is an organization of patients, medical professionals, scientists, and concerned citizens promoting safe and legal access to marijuana for therapeutic use and research. ASA works to overcome political and legal barriers by creating policies that improve access to medical cannabis for patients and researchers through legislation, education, litigation, grassroots actions, advocacy, and services for patients and their care-givers. ASA publishes booklets about the use of cannabis for medical conditions, available at its website.

Cato Institute
1000 Massachusetts Ave. NW, Washington, DC 20001-5403
(202) 842-0200
fax: (202) 842-3490
e-mail: cato@cato.org
website: www.cato.org

The institute is a public policy research foundation dedicated to limiting the control of government and to protecting individual liberty. The Cato Institute strongly favors drug legalization. The institute publishes the *Cato Journal* three times a year and the *Cato Policy Report* bimonthly.

Center for Medicinal Cannabis Research (CMCR)
220 Dickinson St., Ste. B, Mail Code 8231, San Diego, CA 92103-8231
(619) 543-5024
e-mail: cmcr@ucsd.edu
website: www.cmcr.ucsd.edu

CMCR conducts scientific studies intended to ascertain the general medical safety and efficacy of cannabis and cannabis products. CMCR aims to be a resource for health policy planning on the issue of medical marijuana. CMCR provides a list of its published research at its website, with access to select publications.

Drug Free America Foundation, Inc. (DFAF)
5999 Central Ave., Ste. 301, Saint Petersburg, FL 33710
(727) 828-0211
fax: (727) 828-0212
website: www.dfaf.org

DFAF is a drug prevention and policy organization committed to developing, promoting, and sustaining global strategies, policies, and laws that will reduce illegal drug use, drug addiction, drug-related injury, and death. DFAF opposes efforts that would legalize, decriminalize, or promote illicit drugs, including the legalization of medical or recreational marijuana. DFAF publishes several position statements available at its website, including "Marijuana—Questions and Answers."

Drug Policy Alliance (DPA)
70 W. Thirty-Sixth St., 16th Fl., New York, NY 10018
(212) 613- 8020
fax: (212) 613- 8021
e-mail: nyc@drugpolicy.org
website: www.drugpolicy.org

DPA supports and publicizes alternatives to current US policies on illegal drugs, including marijuana. DPA has worked on initiatives in several states to make medical marijuana legally available to patients. DPA publishes many research briefs and fact sheets, such as "Medical Marijuana and Cancer," available at its website.

Marijuana Policy Project (MPP)
PO Box 77492, Capitol Hill, Washington, DC 20013
(202) 462-5747
e-mail: mpp@mpp.org
website: www.mpp.org

MPP works to further public policies that allow for responsible medical and nonmedical use of marijuana and that minimize the harms associated with marijuana consumption and the laws that manage its use. MPP works to increase public support for marijuana regulation and lobbies for marijuana policy reform at the state and federal levels. MPP works to increase public awareness through speaking engagements, educational seminars, the mass media, and briefing papers.

National Institute on Drug Abuse (NIDA)
6001 Executive Blvd., Rm. 5213, MSC 9561, Bethesda, MD 20892-9561
(301) 443-6245
e-mail: information@nida.nih.gov
website: www.nida.nih.gov

NIDA is a part of the National Institutes of Health, a component of the US Department of Health and Human Services, with the mission of using science to address drug abuse and addiction. NIDA supports and conducts research on drug abuse—including the yearly Monitoring the Future Survey—to improve addiction prevention, treatment, and policy efforts. It publishes the bimonthly *NIDA Notes* newsletter, the periodic *NIDA Capsules* fact sheets, and a catalog of research reports and public education materials, such as *Marijuana: Facts for Teens* and *Marijuana: Facts Parents Need to Know.*

National Organization for the Reform of Marijuana Laws (NORML)
1600 K St. NW, Ste. 501, Washington, DC 20006-2832
(202) 483-5500
fax: (202) 483-0057
e-mail: norml@norml.org
website: www.norml.org

NORML's mission is to move public opinion to achieve the repeal of marijuana prohibition so that the responsible use of cannabis by adults is no longer subject to penalty. NORML lobbies state and federal legislators in support of reform legislation, including the end of marijuana prohibition for both medical and personal use. NORML has numerous research and position papers available at its website, including *Rethinking the Consequences of Decriminalizing Marijuana.*

Office of National Drug Control Policy (ONDCP)
Drug Policy Information Clearinghouse, PO Box 6000, Rockville, MD 20849-6000

(800) 666-3332
fax: (301) 519-5212
e-mail: ondcp@ncjrs.org
website: www.whitehousedrugpolicy.gov

ONDCP, a component of the Executive Office of the President, establishes policies, priorities, and objectives for the nation's drug control program. ONDCP works to reduce illicit drug use, manufacturing, and trafficking; drug-related crime and violence; and detrimental drug-related health consequences. ONDCP has numerous publications related to its mission, including *Marijuana Myths & Facts: The Truth Behind 10 Popular Misperceptions.*

Rand Corporation

1776 Main St., Santa Monica, CA 90401-3208
(310) 393-0411
fax: (310) 393-4818
website: www.rand.org

The Rand Corporation is a nonprofit organization that conducts research on important and complicated social problems. The Rand Corporation's Drug Policy Research Center conducts research to help community leaders and public officials develop more effective ways of dealing with drug problems. Its *DPRC Insights* is a regularly published electronic newsletter that focuses on major drug policy issues.

For Further Reading

Books

Benavie, Arthur. *Drugs: America's Holy War.* New York: Routledge, 2009. Argues that an end to the war on drugs would yield enormous benefits, destroy dangerous drug cartels, and allow the government to refocus its attention on public health.

Booth, Martin. *Cannabis: A History.* New York: Picador, 2005. Chronicles the process through which cannabis became outlawed throughout the Western world and the effect such legislation has had on the global economy.

Chapkis, Wendy, and Richard J. Webb. *Dying to Get High: Marijuana as Medicine.* New York: New York University Press, 2008. Through interviews with patients, public officials, law enforcement officers, and physicians, chronicles the complex history of medical marijuana in America.

Earleywine, Mitch. *Understanding Marijuana: A New Look at the Scientific Evidence.* New York: Oxford University Press, 2005. Examines the biological, psychological, and societal impact of marijuana use.

Earleywine, Mitch, ed. *Pot Politics: Marijuana and the Costs of Prohibition.* New York: Oxford University Press, 2007. Presents ethical, religious, economic, psychological, and political arguments for cannabis policies that range from prohibition to unrestricted legalization.

Fox, Steve, Paul Armentano, and Mason Tvert. *Marijuana Is Safer: So Why Are We Driving People to Drink?* White River Junction, VT: Chelsea Green, 2009. Compares and contrasts the relative harms and legal status of the two most popular recreational substances in the world—marijuana and alcohol.

Geluardi, John. *Cannabiz: The Explosive Rise of the Medical Marijuana Industry.* Sausalito, CA: Polipoint, 2010. Chronicles the legalization of medical marijuana in California and fourteen other states, describing challenges faced by the new industry.

Gerber, Rudolph J. *Legalizing Marijuana: Drug Policy Reform and Prohibition Politics*. Westport, CT: Praeger, 2004. Highlights the failures of the government's war on marijuana, likening it to 1920s-style Prohibition politics, and points to the need for citizen initiatives to change drug policy.

Grim, Ryan. *This Is Your Country on Drugs: The Secret History of Getting High in America*. Hoboken, NJ: Wiley, 2010. Traces the evolution of the long US relationship with drugs, commenting on the impact of antidrug policies.

Husak, Doug, and Peter de Marneffe. *The Legalization of Drugs*. New York: Cambridge University Press, 2006. Two philosophers of law debate the issue of drug legalization, taking opposing positions and arguing the merits of each.

Iverson, Leslie L. *The Science of Marijuana*. New York: Oxford University Press, 2007. Explains the advances that have been made in scientific research on cannabis with the discovery of specific receptors and the existence of naturally occurring cannabis-like substances in the brain.

Kuhn, Cynthia, Scott Swartzwelder, and Wilkie Wilson. *Buzzed: The Straight Facts About the Most Used and Abused Drugs from Alcohol to Ecstasy*. 3rd ed. New York: W.W. Norton, 2008. Relays information for understanding how drugs—such as marijuana—affect the body and behavior.

Regan, Trish. *Joint Ventures: Inside America's Almost Legal Marijuana Industry*. Hoboken, NJ: Wiley, 2011. Explores the inner workings of America's exploding marijuana industry and its flourishing underground economy.

Room, Robin, Benedikt Fischer, Wayne Hall, Simon Lenton, and Peter Reuter. *Cannabis Policy: Moving Beyond Stalemate*. New York: Oxford University Press, 2010. Reviews the health effects, trends in use, and legal stances on marijuana, exploring the impacts of various changes in policy.

Periodicals and Internet Sources

American Society of Addiction Medicine (ASAM). "Public Policy Statement on Medical Marijuana," April 2010. www.wfad.se/lat

est-news/1-articles/213-asam-public-policy-statement-on-qmedi
cal-marijuanaq.

Armentano, Paul. "Viewpoints: Prohibition of Pot Feeds Lawlessness," *Sacramento (CA) Bee*, January 10, 2010.

Baltimore Sun. "Marijuana Conundrum," February 1, 2010.

Bandow, Doug. "Arrest Michael Phelps Now!," *National Review*, February 6, 2009.

Beam, Christopher. "Gateway Drug Policy," *Slate*, October 19, 2009. www.slate.com.

Belville, Russ. "Sanjay Gupta: What the Next Surgeon General Doesn't Know About Pot," *AlterNet*, January 8, 2009. www.alternet.org.

Bracken, Richard. "Legalizing Marijuana Just Makes Sense," *St. George (UT) Dixie Sun and Albany (NY) Times Union*, April 11, 2010.

Brannigan, Michael. "Let the Sick Decide if Marijuana Is Medicine," *Times Union* (Albany, NY), March 28, 2010.

Califano, Joseph A., Jr. "Should Drugs Be Decriminalised? No," *BMJ*, November 10, 2007.

Christian Science Monitor. "A Federal Misstep with Medical Marijuana?," October 20, 2009.

Corry, Jessica Peck. "Republican Moms for Marijuana: 'Time to Legalize Is Now,'" *Boulder Colorado Daily*, July 26, 2009.

Corry, Robert J., Jr. "Stop the Medical Marijuana Madness," *Denver Post*, November 2, 2009.

Croke, Bill. "High Under the Big Sky," *American Spectator*, June 2, 2010.

Dixie, Dora, and Pete Bensinger. "Medical Marijuana Is Bad Medicine, Bad Policy," *Arlington Heights (IL) Daily Herald*, June 2, 2010.

Doherty, Brian. "L.A.'s Pot Revolution," *Reason*, May 2010.

DuPont, Robert L. "What's Wrong with Legalizing Illegal Drugs?," Institute for Behavior and Health, March 24, 2009. www.ibhinc.org.

Eddy, Mark. "Medical Marijuana: Review and Analysis of Federal and State Policies," CRS Report for Congress, Congressional Research Service, April 2, 2010. www.fas.org/sgp/crs/misc/RL33211.pdf.

Office of National Drug Control Policy. "National Drug Control Strategy: 2009 Annual Report," January 2009. www.whitehouse drugpolicy.gov/publications/policy/ndcs09/2009ndcs.pdf.

Parker, Kathleen. "Phelps Takes a Hit," *Washington Post*, February 4, 2009.

Parloff, Roger. "How Marijuana Became Legal," *Fortune*, September 18, 2009.

Redman, John. "Health Costs of Legalization Would Outstrip Revenue Gains," *San Diego Union-Tribune*, January 10, 2010.

Soliman, Ahmed. "Don't OK Medical Marijuana Bill," *Record* (Bergen County, NJ), February 27, 2009.

Stein, Joel. "Save the Pot Dealers!," *Time*, November 16, 2009.

Stimson, Charles "Cully." "The Law Is on the Feds' Side," *Los Angeles Times*, April 22, 2008.

Stossel, John. "Legalize All Drugs," *Jewish World Review*, June 18, 2008.

Sullum, Jacob. "Smoking Marijuana Isn't a Harbinger of Ruin," *Los Angeles Times*, April 23, 2008.

Todd, Tamar. "California Is Free to Make Its Own Drug Laws," *Los Angeles Times*, January 14, 2010.

Vlahos, Kelley Beaucar. "Higher Law: Will States' Rights Go Up in Smoke?," *American Conservative*, March 9, 2009.

Waldman, Paul. "Can Reason Win the Drug War?," *American Prospect*, November 3, 2009. www.prospect.org.

Warren, Ray. "Because Marijuana Eradication Policy Is Hopeless, Tax and Regulate Instead," *Los Angeles Daily Journal*, July 19, 2007.

Weiner, Robert S. "The War Is Not Lost," *Washington Post*, August 22, 2007.

Websites

Drug Enforcement Administration (www.justice.gov/dea). This website contains information on US drug policy and links to information about marijuana and other drugs.

Hemp and Cannabis Foundation (http://thc-foundation.com). This website contains information about legal issues related to medical marijuana, medical marijuana clinics, and research on medical uses of marijuana.

Partnership for a Drug-Free America (www.drugfree.org). This website features interactive tools that translate the latest science and research on teen behavior, addiction, and treatment into tips and tools for parents.

Index

Picture Credits

AP Images/Ed Andrieski, 43

AP Images/The Canadian Press, Jonathan Hayward, 113

AP Images/Peter Dejong, 23

AP Images/Lenny Ignentzi, 67

AP Images/LM Otero, 49

AP Images/The Press Democrat/John Burgess, 76

AP Images/US Justice Department Drug Enforcement Agency, 39

AP Images/Richard Vogel, 79

© Catchlight Visual Services/Alamy, 60

Robert Galbraith/Reuters/Landov, 47, 83

Gale, Cengage Learning, 16, 20, 29, 34, 38, 51, 55, 61, 65, 72, 82, 91, 95, 102, 115

G&H Productions / The Kobal Collection, 44

Pascal Goetgheluck/Photo Researchers, Inc., 27

Joshua Gunter/The Plain Dealer/Landov, 96

Aaron Kehoe/UPI/Landov, 71

James Keyser/Time Life Pictures/Getty Images, 56

LADA/Photo Researchers, Inc., 88

Mike Mergen/Bloomberg via Getty Images, 109

Robert Nickelsberg/Getty Images, 100

Victor de Schwanberg/Photo Researchers, Inc., 11

Jim Varney/Photo Researchers, Inc., 33

Tim Vernon/Photo Researchers, Inc., 14